P9-DHA-578

JENNIFER SERRAVALLO

New York Times best-selling author of *The Reading Strategies Book*

Connecting with Students Online

STRATEGIES FOR Remote Teaching & Learning

HEINEMANN, PORTSMOUTH, NH

Heinemann
361 Hanover Street
Portsmouth, NH 03801–3912
www.heinemann.com

Offices and agents throughout the world

Library of Congress Control Number: 2020917084
ISBN: 978-0-325-13229-7

Editor: Katie Wood Ray
Production: Victoria Merecki
Cover and interior designs: Suzanne Heiser
Cover images: © Shutterstock/veronchick_84 *(hand icon);* © Getty Images/Mark Airs *(target)*
Interior art: © Shutterstock/chuckchee/HIP *(web graphic)*
Typesetting: Gina Poirier Design
Video editing: Michael Grover and Sherry Day
Manufacturing: Steve Bernier and Valerie Cooper

Printed in the United States of America on acid-free paper
2 3 4 5 6 7 8 9 10 MPP 25 24 23 22 21 20
October 2020 Printing

Contents

4 Managing Your Time Across a Day, Across the Week 64

STRATEGIES

5 Supporting Students' Independent Practice at Home 82

STRATEGIES

☞ About the Online Resources

In the online resources for this book you will find a variety of videos with and for K–8 students recorded using Zoom, Clips, Loom, and/or Screencastify during the spring and summer of 2020. Some of them were filmed before I had envisioned this book, when I was supporting friends and family with virtual one-on-one and small-group instruction during the early months of the pandemic-initiated shut-down, or as examples for teachers in my Reading and Writing Strategies Facebook Community. A few were filmed during the summer, after school was closed, but children were still trying to continue independent writing projects and book clubs they'd started and enjoyed during spring. The students in the videos are the children of friends, my own children, or neighbors who graciously agreed to join me for some literacy work; I'm not their regular teacher. Though everything here shows examples of teaching and connecting through the screen, the structures you'll learn about in this book (e.g., conferences, minilessons, small-group strategy lessons, and so on) work whether you're in person in a classroom with children, you are working with them virtually, or some hybrid of the two.

How to Access Online Resources

To access online resources for *Connecting with Students Online*:

1. Go to **http://hein.pub/ConnectOnline-login**.
2. Log in with your username and password. If you do not already have an account with Heinemann, you will need to create an account.
3. On the Welcome page, choose

   "Click here to register an Online Resource."
4. Register your product by entering the code: **CWSONL** (be sure to read and check the acknowledgment box under the keycode).
5. Once you have registered your product, it will appear alphabetically in your account list of My Online Resources.

Note: When returning to Heinemann.com to access your previously registered products, simply log into your Heinemann account and click on "View my registered Online Resources."

☞ Video List

Chapter	Description	Other Notes
2	Welcome video	A third-grade teacher welcomes caregivers and families to her online classroom. (3 ½ minutes)
2	Tech support video	A third-grade teacher provides a 90-second tutorial for students and families on how to easily join a Google Meet.
3	Tech support video	A third-grade teacher provides a 90-second tutorial for students and families on how to check comments in Google Docs to read and respond to her feedback.
6	Minilesson: writing, primary	Short minilesson video created with Loom (4 minutes)
6	Minilesson: writing, upper grades	Short minilesson video created with Clips (1 minute)
6	Minilesson: reading, upper grades	Short minilesson video created with Clips (2 minutes)
6	Small-group mentor text study lesson: writing, upper grades	Three rising eighth graders study a mentor text, name craft, and consider what they'll try in their own writing. (7 ½ minutes)
6	Conference: writing, primary	One-on-one conference with a kindergartener (7 ½ minutes)
6	Conference: reading, upper grades	One-on-one conference with a middle schooler (9 minutes)
6	Book club: primary	A first-grade book club discusses a picture book after viewing a recorded read-aloud video. (6 ½ minutes)
6	Book club: upper grades	A fifth-grade book club uses video to converse asynchronously. (5 minutes)
6	Small-group strategy lesson: writing, upper grades	Three fifth-grade students learn a strategy for coming up with their own writing topics and genres for independent projects. (11 ½ minutes)

Acknowledgments

Writing a book is always a collaborative effort. However, this one more than any I've ever written feels like there are other names that deserve to be on the cover alongside mine. It is no exaggeration to say I would have never pulled off this book in such an extremely short timeline without the support and help of many.

To Vicki Boyd for the idea and Roderick Spelman for finding the resources to make it happen: thank you for your belief and trust in me, and for your support.

To Katie Ray, hero of an editor: thank you for telling me that the book would be better if it was completely rewritten after the first draft, when it would have been easier just to pass it through as-is, and then going above and beyond to help me to get it done. You were right, of course! I appreciate your talented eye, your skillful use of a scalpel to trim paragraphs to their essence, and your collaborative spirit. (And by extension, thank you to Jim and your pups for letting this book take over so much of their time with you).

To my colleagues who jumped in to help with content development early on despite the million other things you were juggling, and for contributing in such rich and meaningful ways, I couldn't have done this so quickly without you: Molly Feeney Wood, Barb Golub, Berit Gordon, Lainie Gatch Powell, and Darren Victory.

To my colleagues who shared distance learning experiences and examples, did close and careful reading of early drafts, and provided invaluable feedback, thank you for your reality checks and perspectives: Roseann Maurantonio, Gina Dignon, Gabriel Mercado Ortiz, Raffaella DeMartinis.

Thank you to Patty Adams who pulled off a miracle of a production timeline and for your flexibility with the process. Thank you Sarah Fournier for dropping everything to give this project your full attention, and for taking such care with all the pieces.

Thank you to Heather Anderson for weighing in on key decisions and providing support with research. Thank you Zoë Ryder White for giving the manuscript a careful read-through and providing essential comments that informed revisions.

Victoria Merecki, production editor extraordinaire, thank you for working around the clock to move this project through, and doing it with such a careful detail-oriented eye and calm. You're so calm.

Suzanne Heiser, I don't know how you do it but thank you again for gifting yet another of my books with one of your stunning designs. I appreciate how much care you take to make sure my words and ideas are easy to access. Your design makes the book!

Michael Grover and Sherry Day, thank you for taking such good care of the videos and for editing them with lightning speed.

Eric Chalek, thank you as always for your enthusiasm and support of my work, and for pulling off a campaign to spread the word with such urgency and skill.

Thank you to my family for understanding the importance of this book, and giving me time away from summer play to get it done posthaste.

Introduction

☞ Who Is This Book For?

As I write this, schools throughout the United States and the rest of the world have spent anywhere from three to six months in forced remote instruction because of COVID-19. Some districts are making plans for the 2020–2021 school year, while others are already back to school. Though the plans vary, online instruction will undoubtedly play a role in every one of them, either by design or by necessity as the pandemic forces periods of quarantine.

Truthfully, I hope that the life of this book is short—that scientists deliver a vaccine soon, and that we can all get back into classrooms with students to learn in person. Until then, what we've learned from the past few months is that connection is crucial for our students and for us, and I hope this book helps teachers who want to find ways to connect, to hold true to research-based principles of good teaching, and who are looking for practical support to bring their classroom interactions and community online in ways that are beneficial to students and not overtaxing to teachers or caregivers. What I offer in this book is one vision for how to make this possible; I offer it knowing that we will all continue to learn together, share, and innovate with online learning in the months ahead.

No matter what model your district has chosen, or what needs to happen to keep everyone safe as the year progresses, here are some ways this book may be of help to you:

All Online	
Schools offering an all-remote option, or teachers assigned to run a class fully online	This book will help you with all aspects of the job, from establishing connections and community in online spaces (Chapter 1), to partnering with caregivers (Chapter 2), to planning streamlined accessible curriculum (Chapter 3), scheduling (Chapters 4 and 5), and transferring various balanced literacy structures to the online space (Chapter 6).

Intermittent Periods of Online	
Schools that are all in person, but need to shift to online instruction when suspected or confirmed cases of COVID crop up and the class needs to go into quarantine	Even though you're starting out in person, establishing strong communities with a trauma-informed approach and partnering with caregivers will be crucial foundational work (Chapters 1 and 2). Setting up an online classroom Learning Management System from the beginning will be crucial to make the transition to all-online learning possible. Storing key classroom charts, recorded lessons, rubrics and skill progressions, and more will allow for a more seamless transition to at-home learning for students. Advice about unit planning and simplifying and streamlining will also be valuable in even an in-person, socially distanced classroom, and simplifying things now will make transitions to online go more smoothly (Chapter 3). You can think about what children will need at home, and empty out classroom library shelves and writing centers as soon as you know you will be shifting to learning at home to set students up for independent practice (Chapter 5). During the at-home period, you'll want to generously borrow ideas from the parts of the book that describe methods of instruction (Chapter 6) and how to schedule your time (Chapter 4). Look at them now, even though your students are in person with you, and consider what tech tools, norms, and routines might be good to establish and teach now as any shift to all online is likely to be unplanned and abrupt. The more you can do now to prepare for it, the more seamless the transition will be for you and your students. Consider also preparing parents for the possibility, and do some work with them now to help them get ready (Chapter 2).

Hybrid Models

Schools where children will be coming to school in-person five days a week for half days, with online learning happening each afternoon Or **Districts where children will spend a couple days each week in school and a couple days each week at home** Or **Districts where some children will be in school in person, a camera in the classroom livestreams the happenings to those at home, and the teacher manages both simultaneously**	The first chapter is about staying focused on priorities, emphasizing trauma-informed approaches sensitive to social-emotional well-being, and building community. This will be important no matter how many hours or days children are with you in the classroom (and in truth, it's something that should happen even if we are fully in school buildings). Partnering with caregivers (Chapter 2) will be essential whether you're in person or online or toggling between the two. Setting up clear expectations for work at home and communicating clearly, among other things, will help make transitions smoother. Advice about simplifying and streamlining unit planning will be valuable as children and you alternate between an in-person, socially distanced classroom and online learning. Time will be lost in transitions, and simplifying and clarifying curricular goals now will make transitions go more smoothly (Chapter 3). You'll want to consider what you can do in person with children off devices, what lessons and activities you'll still want to do with devices even though you're in person, and which lessons and activities you'll save for the online portion of students' week or day (Chapters 5 and 6). For example, even if children are in person for a portion of the time, the fact that they must remain distanced makes book clubs, conferences, strategy lessons, and more very challenging. Therefore, you might choose to run small groups and conferences when you're connecting with children online and do the whole-class (read-aloud, minilessons) and independent practice portions (Chapter 5) while students are in the classroom. You can also take advantage of the children being with you in person to provide them with supplies and books to take home for continued practice. Additionally, you might find using some of the tools described in this book, such as shared e-documents, to work well in a socially distanced classroom, because instead of going over to a student (still six feet apart) as they write, you can comment in real time and chat by typing in their e-document to give feedback and converse. The advice about managing time and scheduling (Chapters 4 and 5) may help you think about how to balance time and balance activities, though you'll likely begin by blocking out sections of your day for in-person and at-home instruction.

☞ Is This a Book About Technology?

In the spring when everyone went to remote instruction, my first thought was, "I need to figure out some more apps, platforms, and tech tools." Perhaps you can relate? My first effort to support teachers was to interview Katie Muhtaris and Kristin Ziemke, authors of helpful and practical books about digital literacy and incorporating technology (*Amplify* [2015], *Read the World* [2019]). Although maybe I expected them to teach me about a dozen new tech tools, the advice they shared instead was so helpful, and true: keep it simple. The technology is a tool.

They aren't the only ones with that opinion. For example, Harvard University's "Teach Remotely—Best Practices for Online Pedagogy" states:

> *Focus on your pedagogy, not the medium: the principles of pedagogy that are effective for online teaching . . . are similar to those that are effective in the residential classroom. They allow students to engage with material dynamically and across multiple learning styles. These principles apply not only to synchronous teaching but also, importantly, to asynchronous content creation.*

Focusing too much on tech takes us away from what really matters—how you are teaching and connecting with students. Also, it's overwhelming for you, students, and parents when you incorporate too many different tools with different log-ins, passwords, bells and whistles, especially if these tech tools are ones that children (and/or you!) didn't already know how to use

TECH TIP

Be sure to explicitly teach children how to use any new tech tool, app, and so on that you plan to use for remote instruction; record a video for adults who are supporting students at home to teach what it is and how it functions; and provide support for the first week or so when students are using it.

independently. And if you work with middle school students who have multiple teachers, it's better for students and families if you all get on the same page with the few tools you'll use.

I think it's best to get to know and use a small handful of tools that can serve many purposes and use them over and over again for a while until everyone is as comfortable with them as you are with email and texting. Only then should you consider trying a new one (but only if you want to!).

Throughout Chapters 2 through 6 you will see boxes titled "Tech Nuts and Bolts" when there is technology to consider alongside the teaching strategy described. In these boxes I offer examples of tools, or tips about ways to use a tool, that are simple and effective to accomplish the teaching, learning, and assessing I describe. These are just suggestions; you may already be familiar with a different tool that does the same job, or your district may have set parameters around what apps and platforms you are allowed to use. You'll also notice I follow my own advice—you'll see me mention the same handful of tools that I know can do a lot and that I use over and over for many different purposes.

In the table on the following page, I've listed the main things you'll need to be able to do with online teaching to share content, connect with students, engage them, and collect feedback. Next to each are some examples of widely available, often free tools (that you'll see mentioned throughout this book) that help with that job. Choose one from each box, or pick a different one that serves the same purpose, but whatever you do, don't try to learn too many new tools at once.

Classroom Platform/Learning Management System (LMS) or Organization System (choose one!)	**Videoconferencing** (choose one!)
Examples Google Classroom Canvas Schoology Class Blog	*Examples* Zoom Google Meet GoToMeeting Microsoft Teams FaceTime Google Hangouts
Lesson Recording (choose one at first, maybe add a second one as you become comfortable)	**Asynchronous Communication** (choose one at first, maybe add more as you become comfortable)
Examples Screencastify Clips Screencast-O-Matic Loom Zoom	*Examples* Email Seesaw Flipgrid Google Forms Google Docs Texting/Direct Messaging Padlet Marco Polo
Audiobooks, Podcasts (optional, use if book access is challenging)	**Texts** (optional, use if book access is challenging)
Examples Overdrive Stitcher Apple Podcasts Audible	*Examples* Libby Epic! ReadWorks Newsela Scholastic Trueflix YouTube (videos of texts being read aloud) Storyline Online Capstone Interactive Reading A to Z

Other
(optional—remember, fit the tool to the purpose!)

Jamboard—create a collaborative whiteboard/online bulletin board

Toy Theater—use online manipulatives for math, phonics, and more

Edpuzzle—create your own interactive video lessons

Google Docs—create hyper-documents with many links to assignments or sites, organized in one place

Mentimeter—poll students live and share results in real time

iDocCam— turn your phone into a document camera

SurveyMonkey—elicit feedback from students and/or caregivers

Sign Up Genius—create a schedule with open timeslots, auto-send reminders

Calendy—sign up for meetings with automatic integration with various online calendars and videoconferencing platforms such as Zoom

Chapter 1

Holding True to Priorities as We Move Online

Teachers across the country heroically sprang into action during the first period of COVID-19 quarantine in spring 2020, engaging in what some have called *crisis teaching* or *emergency teaching* (Milman 2020). This experience put a spotlight on a number of real equity and access problems "in our school systems—and in our society—that too many of us have allowed to exist without question" with vast differences in students' abilities to have access to a device, connect to Wi-Fi, or even have the books or food they need and more (Simmons 2020). We experienced challenges with trying to teach, reach, and engage children, especially young children, children with special needs, and multilingual students (Reich 2020a; Mitchell 2020; Stewart 2020; Hill 2020). On the other hand, for some students, being able to work at home, at their own pace, and on their own schedules turned out to be beneficial and positive (Gray 2020). We all learned a lot.

This book is a quick effort to organize, synthesize, and elaborate on the support I began offering teachers through social media, blogging, and webinars during that time. In this book I offer advice from the perspective of someone who has taught adults (teachers) virtually for more than a decade through online courses and webinars, as a parent who had a first and fifth grader on the learning end of remote instruction last spring, and as a teacher who supported K–8th grade children of neighbors and family through individual and small-group instruction online during the spring and summer. I also learned a great deal from my colleagues overseas in Europe and throughout Asia who shared countless lessons learned from their days of remote instruction which began in early 2020, and from teachers throughout the United States who joined me in think tanks and collaborated with me as we learned about this together.

As we embark on the continuation of remote instruction this school year, I have no doubt we will continue to learn, revise, adjust, and grow. New research will come out. Educators will innovate and create and share. However, regardless of new technology, new Learning Management Systems, or new ideas for engaging kids online, we would be wise to hold fast to research-based essential elements of learning—principles that are true whether we are in person or online—and apply what we can to the virtual space. In this chapter I offer eight priorities that are the foundational underpinnings of the fifty-five-plus practical instructional strategies offered throughout this book:

- Connection and Relationships
- Emotional Well-Being
- Engagement
- Clear, Strategic, and Focused Direct Instruction
- Guided Practice
- Access
- Assessment
- Balance

☞ Connection and Relationships

In spring 2020, many teachers reported feeling like their teaching was going out into a void. They missed their students' smiles and hugs and the looks on their faces when light bulbs went on. Students missed their friends and teachers. With forced distancing for the sake of public health, many felt isolated and alone. It's one of the things that many fear most about returning to online instruction: losing the connection and community that exists in the classroom.

As we know from Howard, McCall, and Howard (2020), "Learning requires a relationship." Building trust, knowing students and caregivers well and making sure they know you, prioritizing relationships, and doing all of this in a culturally responsive and sustaining way is a crucial foundation to helping children to engage and work toward academic goals, whether we are in a classroom or online together (Hammond 2014). Decades of research has shown that positive school and classroom cultures are crucial for learning, and recent research has shown positive culture to be correlated with successfully moving their classrooms online (Cohen et al. 2009; Hoffman, Brackett, and Levy 2020; National School Climate Center 2007; Greenberg 2020).

Build Strong Relationships with and Between Students

Relationship-building begins by welcoming and honoring students' identities; children need to know it's safe to be their true selves and share who they are with you and with the class (Muhammad 2020; Minor 2018; Ahmed 2018; Howard, McCall, and Howard 2020). As Krause (2020) writes, "Online learning is most effective when everyone belongs. It hinges on relational trust, and your job, in part, is to keep the foundation on safety and inclusion."

Ahmed 2018

One way to do this is to spend time inviting children to create identity webs and/or heart maps to share, find connections, and learn more about each other (Ahmed 2018; Heard 2016). Think about and draw from other routines and practices that helped you get to know students better in the classroom, such as interest surveys, playing games, or leading morning circle. Once you know your learners, you can make what you teach and how you teach identity affirming.

Connect with students individually or in small groups as often as your schedule allows (Reich 2020a, 2020b; Flaherty 2020; Greenberg 2020). Establish and keep predictable times for morning meeting/circle, book shares or other share-outs, small-group and one-on-one conferences, check-ins, and more. By treating these opportunities for connection as regularly scheduled events, not an irregular option, you will really know your students and what they need (see more in Chapters 4 and 6). You matter: research has shown that students are able to overcome difficult events and shield themselves from anxiety when they have at least one supportive adult in their lives (Brooks 2003). As Minahan (2020) writes, "A connection with a caring teacher can be a lifeline for a vulnerable student" (23).

Take time outside of academics to connect with children on a personal level. Try to find at least one thing you have in common that is not school related—a love of dogs? A hobby of baking? A favorite sports team? Then share with children about these interests regularly. Invite children to respond to the prompt, "I wish my teacher knew . . ." to express something that will help you get to know them better.

Anna

I wish my teacher knew that I am proud to be weird. And that I am obsessed with anime shows and video games. And that I am a blue belt in taekwondo. I wish my teacher knew that I DO pay attention when I'm doodling. And that I only like tuna sushi. I wish my teacher knew that at home, I like to jump on the furniture. And that cats are the main thing I think about all day.

If possible, consider making in-person, socially distanced visits to your students' homes, possibly with a care package of books or other materials they'll need for successful at-home learning (see more in Chapter 5).

Finally, find ongoing ways to help children connect with each other and facilitate their meetups without you there (Reich 2020a, 2020b; Hoffman, Brackett, and Levy 2020; Greenberg 2020). Set up book clubs, writing clubs, and number talks;

utilize breakout rooms for turn-and-talks and small-group conversation; and make sure to teach students how to be engaged participants. (See more about these and other ideas in Chapter 6.)

Build Strong Relationships with Caregivers

Reaching out to make connections and build relationships with caregivers will go a long way.

Remember what's going on in families' lives and reach out with expressions of care—ask about how the new baby has been sleeping at night, if their grandmother has gotten out of the hospital yet, how their virtual dance recital went.

Invite families to share about cultures, backgrounds, traditions, and celebrations, possibly by joining in a class meeting, recording them teaching or sharing something, or inviting them to share photographs and captions on a virtual bulletin board (Souto-Manning and Martell 2016; Hoffman, Brackett, and Levy 2020).

Create a space in your online Learning Management Platform or class blog and/or time in your class or small-group meetings to share what students and families are doing at home so they can celebrate each other together, as a community. Invite families to send in photos to celebrate milestones like a lost tooth, learning to ride a bike, mastering a cartwheel; photos of children working in their at-home work environments; videos of children sharing their published writing or reading to a younger sibling.

Caregivers will be invaluable partners, so keeping communication clear and compassionate, while being supportive and realistic, will be key (read more about partnering with caregivers in Chapter 2) (Hoffman, Brackett, and Levy 2020).

Build Strong Relationships with Other Caring Adults

Reach out to others who may be involved with your students and set up communication systems to make staying in touch easier. For example, communicate with social workers who may be doing regular wellness checks for your students and are making sure they have what they need in terms of supplies and food (Minahan 2020; Hoffman, Brackett, and Levy 2020). Connect and stay in touch with any additional support providers such as special education teachers and physical and occupational therapists to make sure your work with students is aligned. Think through how paraprofessionals and/or classroom aides can support your students. Keep the lines of communication open and consistent so no one slips through the cracks. (See more about developing note-taking and communication systems on pages 22–23.)

☞ Emotional Well-Being

Children's experiences so far with this pandemic and with remote instruction have not been universal. Their realities run the gamut from food insecurity or loved ones getting ill or dying to feeling safe and cared for at home and possibly even making more progress than they would if they were at school. As Kelly Wickham Hurst (2020), Dr. Bettina Love (2019), and Dr. Kim Parker (2020) have pointed out, schools can be damaging to some children because of racism, bullying, or otherwise unsafe school environments, and when students went home to learn they may have actually thrived. Other children may have found that being able to wake up naturally rather than by alarm, and having the freedom to manage their own workflow in a way that suits them, resulted in increased productivity.

We know that the health crisis has disproportionately impacted Black and indigenous communities and communities of color (Godoy and Wood 2020). We can assume that children will have varying levels of awareness of the political climate and protests against police brutality, and these events will impact them in different ways. With these of-the-moment potential stressors and challenges, along with the stress and trauma many children experience on a regular basis, it's clear we need to put care first. We do not teach in a vacuum—now, or ever. We must always work to understand the context in which children are learning, take that context into consideration, and support students' well-being as well as their academic needs.

Professor and educational consultant Alex Shevrin Venet (2016) reminds us to teach with the effects of trauma in mind, always. This doesn't mean we should label or marginalize anyone as a victim of trauma, but that we need to put trauma-informed practices in place that will benefit all students and communities and offer them a chance to recover and heal as they learn (Newhouse 2020). She recommends that we:

- Keep things as **predictable** as possible.
- Stay **flexible.** Be sure kids have what they need, knowing needs will vary.
- **Connect.** Build and maintain relationships above all else.
- **Empower** students so they can face inevitable challenges to come.

Take Care of Yourself

Just as you care deeply about your students' well-being, you need to prioritize your own health to give your students what they need. Your students need you to be fit, rested, and well so you can model healthy ways to be in a challenging world, and so you have the patience and energy to teach.

For each of us, self-care may look different. For some it may mean starting the day with a run, or yoga in the living room. For others, it might be the routine of a shower and cup of tea. For others, it might be calling to check in on Grandma, or doing a floor puzzle with your four-year-old. Many of us (myself included!) need to set a clearly scheduled stop to the work day, and communicate that stop to students and families. Most of us would do well to have a dedicated work space that can be closed off or a place to put away work materials to signal the end of the work day.

Self-care is such a crucial foundation to being able to show up for students that Berit Gordon dedicates an entire chapter to it in her new book, *The Joyful Teacher* (2020). She suggests finding mentors and buddies you can count on for check-ins and supports—folks who really "get" you and give you energy. She also shares an idea called the Pomodoro Technique, where you chunk tasks into manageable pieces (say twenty minutes), set a timer, dive in, take a break when the timer's up, then repeat.

Your students deserve happy and healthy adults in their lives. When you prioritize your needs, it's not taking away from students. It's letting them experience your best teaching self. The more you model self-care and time management, the more you show students the way to protecting their own health and happiness, too.

☞ Engagement

Hollinghead and Carr-Chellman (2019) write, "The quality of student engagement correlates directly with the quality of student learning: An engaged student learns better. While convenience, accessibility, and flexibility attract many students to online learning, the learning environment can be alienating if not thoughtfully designed."

During the spring, some teachers reported children not logging in for lessons at all, or during lessons, turning off cameras or disappearing out of the room. Others held office hours, but struggled to get students to take advantage of them. Still others weren't always sure if children were really doing the work that was assigned. And this may surprise you—but some of your students might have completed every single assignment, got perfect scores, turned it all in on time, and yet were not engaged. They were doing as told, but they were just checking off boxes to get it done.

When I polled teachers to ask what their biggest questions are about continuing remote instruction, 2,876 responded "how to better engage students." It's an important concern. As I wrote a decade ago, "Without engagement, we've got nothing" (2010).

As you probably learned quickly, you have to actively work to engage students in lessons, whether you are on live with them or they are watching a recorded lesson, and work to engage them in independent practice (more on this in Chapters 5 and 6). It's also important to reflect on the authenticity of the assignments you are asking children to do and how relevant the curriculum is to them, and plan with the Universal Design for Learning in mind so all children can access the content (more on this in Chapter 3) (Rappolt-Schlichtmann 2020).

We know that engagement isn't about making children do what we tell them to or being held accountable; it's about helping students to be motivated and inspired. Engagement isn't just about *time on task;* it's about tapping into an emotional commitment to students' goals for learning.

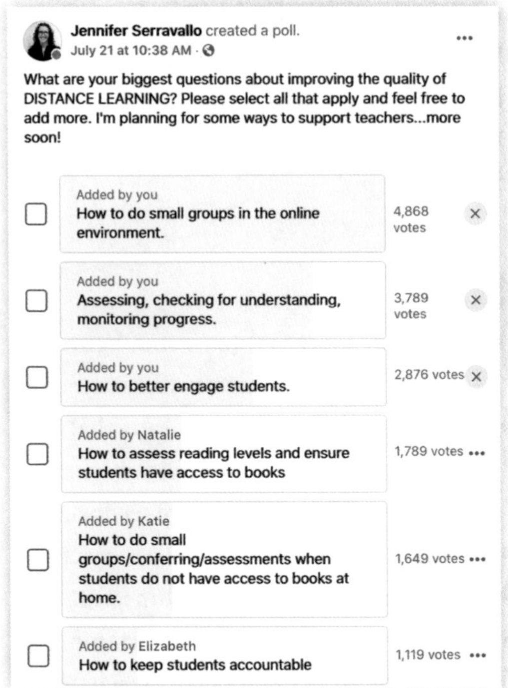

I polled teachers in my Reading and Writing Strategies Facebook Community on July 21, 2020. Small-group instruction, monitoring progress, and engagement were top of mind, and, as you'll read throughout this book, are all interrelated.

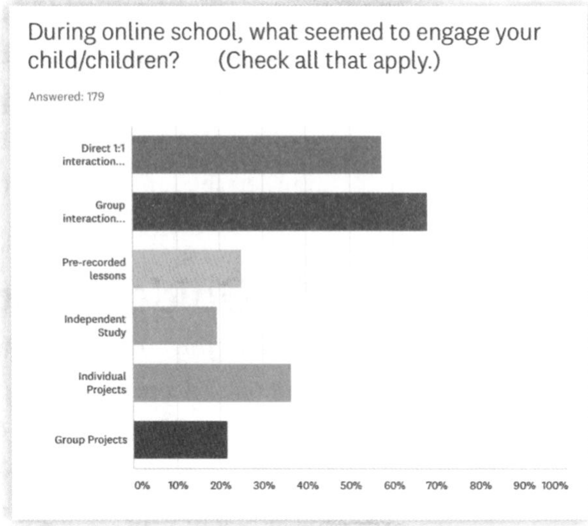

I polled hundreds of parents to ask them about what was most engaging for their children. Notice group and direct one-to-one interaction were most valuable.

Methods *matter*—how you present content, keep learning active, keep learning social, and provide regular opportunities to interact with students to help them engage (more on that in Chapter 6). Additionally, we will all need to be flexible and creative and understand that what engages one learner may not engage another.

☞ Clear, Strategic, and Focused Direct Instruction

Having a clear focus on goals and skills (the *what*) and strategies (the *how*) is crucial as you design your curriculum and as you identify what each individual student needs.

Each of the different methods described in Chapter 6 include naming the strategy clearly, demonstrating or explaining it, and then guiding children to practice it. Strategies are an important ingredient in making your teaching focused, direct, and explicit, and making the learning transferrable, and the skill doable.

☞ Guided Practice

Whether you are working with children in a large group, a small group, or in one-on-one lessons, whether you are teaching in person or through the screen, students benefit from *guided* practice. Guided means that you catch them in the moment of applying a strategy and you point it out to them in a way that is helpful—either offering clear corrective feedback, or redirecting them and helping them to correct an error to help learning stick (Rosenshine 2012; Herrmann 2014; Hattie and Clarke 2018; Hammond 2014). During the initial period of crisis teaching, many teachers reported that simply posting recorded lessons and assignments made them feel disconnected from students' learning; they longed for ways to help learners as they practiced. Chapter 6 will offer you many different high-impact techniques, methods, and tools to guide students and provide feedback as they practice, even when the learning is happening online.

Goals, Skills, and Strategies *Explained*

Goals: A large category. Something that a student can work toward for several weeks. Goals can include multiple skills.

Skills: A proficiency, something a student is able to do.

Strategies: A strategy is a step-by-step how-to. A strategy is not a single word or phrase; rather it is a series of steps. After the student is skilled, the need to apply conscious attention to the strategy fades away.

☞ Access

Universal Design for Learning acknowledges that learners are diverse in terms of background, needs, and interests, and that by eliminating barriers teachers help all students engage and learn (Rappolt-Schlichtmann 2020; Minor 2018). We need to be sure our curriculum, tasks, and materials are carefully considered to allow every unique learner access, we must be flexible and varied with the ways we work with students, and we must offer them different ways to represent what they know, all while holding them to high expectations (see more in Chapters 3 and 6).

It is a misunderstanding that for things to be fair, they need to be exactly the same for each student. In addition to our curriculum and teaching, we have to remember that *how* students learn in their home environments will be incredibly varied; some will have the undivided attention of a family member to help them with everything, while others live with multiple siblings and caregivers who are continuing to work—either remotely or outside the home—and can't assist much if at all. Students have little control over their circumstances at home, so differentiation and flexibility are essential—both in methods and with the frequency of our instruction. Students will need a balance of both whole-class instruction and individualized support, choices in what they read and write, and varying levels of support to access materials to do it all well (see Chapters 5 and 6).

☞ Assessment

Many commonly used assessments and measures of student growth are impractical or invalid when used virtually or remotely. A silver lining to all the ways education was uprooted overnight may likely be a reduced focus on high-stakes, standardized testing that has been problematic, racist, and costly (Rosales 2018; Kendi 2016).

As teachers, we still need to know what students know and are able to do to help us craft and revise unit plans, and that our long hours spent online and in Zoom check-ins, or planning and recording video, are making a difference. We need some way to gauge our impact and understand students' needs and growth so we can adapt accordingly.

The good news is that it's possible and doable to assess and monitor progress with formative assessments and by incorporating techniques during instruction, even though *how* you gather data and determine what students know and are able to do, and what they are ready for next will look different when you're not able to physically listen in on a group or sit next to a student for a running record. In Chapters 3 and 6, you'll see ways to design assessments, collect work, observe students in action, and deliver feedback in a virtual format.

☞ Balance

We moved our classrooms online not by design, but by necessity. If we were teachers in schools that were *designed* to be online schools, we'd have had more time to plan how it would go, participate in ongoing professional development about how to do it well, and at the very least have had child care arranged for our own children. Instead, we are juggling the many challenges that come with living during a pandemic while also trying to teach.

I hope you will find that the advice I offer in this book makes sense and is realistic given the context of the pandemic. My goal is to offer you ways to prioritize, streamline, teach effectively, and support your students' learning so they all grow, but in ways that also ensure you keep your wits about you and you don't overtax caregivers supporting students at home.

What we're after is *balance*. Balance between our own needs and those of our students. Balance between core content areas and foundational skills. Balance between synchronous and asynchronous instruction. Balance between time spent on-screen and time spent off.

What we're after is balance. Between our needs and those of our students, between synchronous and asynchronous instruction, between time spent on-screen and off.

Chapter 2

Partnering with Adults at Home

Schools that are fully online by design (see, for example, K12 and Connections Academy) make clear that someone at home needs to be involved on the student's end for maximum success; the younger the student, the more support from an adult at home they'll require (Kamenetz 2020). Your students' caregivers, though, didn't sign up for online school. Many would prefer for their children to be safely in a classroom with you, and for things to be back to normal; many have mountains of other responsibilities and stressors. On the other hand, some may appreciate watching their children learn and the opportunity to gain greater insight into how to better help them, and may value the increased communication and relationship they can build with their child's teacher.

So although you need to partner with families, it's important to temper expectations for how much they can be involved, differentiate depending on the household, respect caregivers' time, and as a general rule don't assign things that require them to teach. The goal is to make all adults in your students' homes, regardless of their ability to be involved, feel like a welcome part of the classroom. Make sure they all know that you are there to do all the teaching, to help when they need it, that you care, and that you are committed to working together with them to help their child succeed this year (Venet 2016).

Advocacy is also important. The pandemic has further exposed—and exacerbated—the vast gaps in students' access to resources outside of school that were already very real. Everything from food security to health care and more may impact students' experiences, many of which are beyond your control and families' control. What you can do is to advocate for your students and families to ensure that they are aware of resources available to them and that they get what they've been promised. For example, don't assume that a district robocall was received by all, or that the packet of texts and assignments the school announced they mailed was received by all who needed it. As the teacher, you're an important link between the district and the families in your class.

Teaching has always been an art, and as you move online it's an even more delicate balance that demands flexibility and connection with your students and their caregivers.

Welcome Caregivers to Your Online Classroom

Why is this important?

Many caregivers are understandably anxious about remote instruction. What many experienced in the spring was less than ideal. Every new teacher brings new expectations, routines, and ways of doing things. Their children are growing and changing and may respond to remote learning in new and expected ways. They may not be confident in their own abilities to support their children's schoolwork. It's a lot, but you can help put them at ease with a warm welcome to you and your online classroom.

How do I do it?

In a welcome video, just be yourself, communicate some important information, but don't overwhelm with too much detail. Keep it short, and remember your goal is make caregivers feel comfortable partnering with you. Here are a few key points you might share:

- Caregivers are not expected to homeschool their children: you are the teacher and you'll provide carefully planned lessons, feedback, and opportunities for guided practice.
- Independence is key. Students need opportunities to do their own work, that's how they learn and grow, and you'll work hard to make sure assignments are appropriate for each student so they shouldn't need much help from anyone at home.

- Your role isn't to correct all of your students' work with a red pen, but to teach them strategies focused on targeted goals to help them as readers/writers/mathematicians.
- Process is just as important as product.
- Learners need to be flexible, and caregivers should encourage problem solving in children just as you do in the classroom. You might share some of the language you teach students to use to help them solve their own problems.
- Time—and how students will spend it—is on everyone's mind. You might talk about how long students should read, how many pages they should write, how many breaks they might need, and how many hours all of their schoolwork should take.

VIDEO 2.1
Watch a short video welcome from a third-grade teacher.

What are some challenges?

Sometimes grown-ups think their children need help with every little thing and then they come to find out later that the child was asking for help that they didn't really need. Other times, students might ask parents for help with their work when what they actually need is a hug or a snack or some attention, not strategies for long division. And still other times, the work you ask students to do *is* too hard for them. Invite caregivers to keep you in the loop about their child's responses so you can adjust assignments or your support, or offer other strategies. Make it clear that your goal is for children to be doing the work, not their caregivers.

Survey Students and Families to Understand Needs

Why is this important?

To work toward equity (each child gets what they need), you'll need to determine students' access, and gaps in access, to resources. Surveying students and their caregivers early on helps you understand their home learning environment.

How do I do it?

Ideally, you'll have a conversation (by phone or Zoom) with students and/or families, but this could also happen in a written survey. Ask questions that you think will give you the information you need. Be aware that some students' and/or caregivers' most comfortable language might not be English, and reach out to supports in your district to have a translator join you for a call or translate your survey, and invite students and caregivers to respond in whatever language(s) they prefer.

What are some challenges?

Asking these questions in the fall with families you've yet to develop a relationship with may be more challenging than it was last spring. Make sure students and caregivers know that they can trust you to keep what you learn confidential; your goal is to support them with whatever they need to help children succeed. No judgments, only support.

Examples of Questions You Might Ask Students

- Do you need my help getting anything you need to be successful (device, Wi-Fi, printer, paper, etc.)?
- Where do you think you'll do your work? Would you like me to help you think that through?
- What time of day do you like to do your school work?
- How do you like to learn?
- What worked for you last year during remote learning? What didn't?
- Let's talk about books. What do you have at home? Do you have access to the library? What can I do to make sure you have the books you need?
- What else should I know?

Examples of Questions You Might Ask Caregivers

- What's the best way for me to communicate with you?
- What language would you like communications to be in?
- What time of day would be best for me to be available if you need to reach out for help?
- What worked for your child last year during remote learning? What didn't?
- Are there other children at home who will also need help? What are their ages?
- How comfortable are you with the following apps, websites, and learning platform systems? [List those you'll use most.] I will record short videos for any you want or need help with so you're comfortable.
- Do you need help getting the breakfasts and lunches provided by the district?
- What else should I know?

Share the Weekly Schedule

Why is it important?

Like all of us, caregivers are sifting through the ever-changing news cycles, adjusting to new regimens in the workplace, all while they have their children home all day. Careful planning is critical, and what you have planned for their children on any given day is a *major* consideration. They need to know ahead of time.

How do I do it?

Communication about schedules should be regular, consistent, clear, and in a format most accessible to and preferred by families. Research has found that even with Learning Management Systems (LMS) in place, caregivers often prefer email; check with caregivers to see what they prefer (Laho 2019). You might consider sending out an email once a week with a summary of the student work for the week ahead, any upcoming deadlines, as well as all necessary hyperlinks to join scheduled lessons. Don't overwhelm the communication with too much detail—consider using bullets and easily accessible graphics. Try to keep the format of the weekly schedule updates consistent so caregivers can focus only on the content from week to week. Remember to have communications translated if necessary.

TIP

If you have a blog or LMS, save all your weekly schedule updates there (or in some other central location) so caregivers can find and review them easily. Just as you work to provide multiple points of access to students, this is important for caregivers as well.

Ms. Maurantonio's Classroom News

MARCH 16, 2020

Dear Families,

During reading workshop, we will learn to think about our characters by:

- identifying the main character or characters in their books
- using words to describe their characters
- imagining what characters might be thinking
- noticing how characters change.

Encourage your child to read their independent books, mark pages with sticky notes, and share them with you, a friend, a relative, pet, or stuffed animal! I'll check their thinking and give help during conferences. You might also take a photo of your child with their sticky note and send it to me—I'll share these on the class blog!

During writing workshop, we will learn ways to elaborate on (or tell more about) our reasons that are part of our persuasive writing. We will learn that writers might write follow-up sentences that:

- tell stories ("One time . . .")
- "knock the others down" ("The others . . .").

We will also take time to review:

- periods and capital letters
- stretching out words and using what they learned in phonics to help them spell.

Please make sure that children do their own work!! No need to edit for them; I don't expect perfection! The goal is for your child to be able to implement strategies independently over time. Encourage them to use the helper pages I have provided.

During math workshop, we will learn to:

- Add three numbers.
- Add double-digit numbers with a single-digit number with stacking (e.g., 34 + 2).
- Add double-digit numbers with tens and zero ones (e.g., 30 + 20).

Please make sure that they have their base ten blocks and whiteboard ready for our Google Meet calls. We will do problem solving together!

If you ever have any questions, comments, or concerns, please feel free to email me at _____ or reach out to me during office hours (2–3 pm each day).

Stay well!

Share Notes on Students' Work and Progress

Why is this important?

Sharing notes with adults at home shows them that you understand the important role that they play to support students' growth in between lessons. Shared notes also help other teachers who are working with a child to best know how to support them.

How do I do it?

I'm going to pull from one of the best examples of this I've seen to advise you here. My children have been taking piano and voice lessons with their music teachers during home quarantine. One of the systems their music school put in place was a communication system required for all teachers to follow—it's simple but it works so well. The consistent way that both teachers shared information made it easy for me to check up on and monitor my daughters' weekly practice.

- Each teacher sets up a shared document (they used Google Docs).
- Within twenty-four hours of the conclusion of a lesson, the teacher dates the notes, then provides some positive feedback on strides they have made since their last lesson, a review of key items they worked on in the lesson, and some suggestions for the student's practice in the week ahead.
- In addition to the notes, inside the file are links to any supporting material the student might need: audio files, a video strategy lesson (e.g., a demonstration of how to incorporate both hands with "Ode to Joy"),

TIP

If you teach multiple subjects to one class of children, it might be helpful for each child to have *one* document where you share notes for all subjects. For children who learn from multiple teachers, if everyone can get on the same page with a shared note-taking form it's sure to simplify the communication for caregivers.

visuals to support the concepts they are learning (e.g., a pneumonic device to remember what notes are on the lines and spaces in the treble and bass clefs), sheet music, and so on.

- The teacher has editing privileges; caregivers and students can view or comment only.
- We sometimes also use this document to turn stuff back to the teacher; for example, my daughter recently recorded herself playing a whole song and sent the audio file back to the teacher so she could listen.

What I find so helpful is that everything is in one place and is so clear: the feedback (positive and corrective), expectations for independent practice, and any supporting materials. Also, although I nudge my kids to practice, I never feel like I have to be their teacher. (And thank goodness, because I cannot read music, sing, or play piano to save my life!)

7/9/2020:

- **C Position Warm-Up:** Practice with both hands, first separately and eventually at the same.
- C Chord and Octave - New music terms from this lesson!
- Red Book - We'll keep checking out the "Get Ready for Take-Off" section in the first several pages next time!
- **Ode To Joy:** Practice the LH bass clef notes we went over and see if you can start trying both hands together at the same time!

7/16/2020:

- **C Position Warm-Up:** Now that you're doing well at playing this with each hand separately, try practicing with both hands at the same time. This is a bit confusing because you'll start with RH 1-finger on C at the same time as LH 5-finger on C (i.e. the fingering won't match up, but you'll be playing the same notes an octave apart in either hand). This will be an important first step in getting our hands to work together when we play the piano!
- **Ode To Joy:** [Video link next page] Now that we've figured out all the LH notes, it's time to begin practicing both hands at the same time. Try circling all the notes that happen together at the same time on your sheet music to help you with a visual aid. Here's a picture for an example:

- **New Song! Brother John:** Practice this new song we learned by ear ("Are you sleepy" etc). Here is some sheet music to help remind you of the notes.

Grant Richards, Mark Murphy Music

Record How-To Videos for Using Technology

Why is this important?

You can't assume that caregivers have the same experience that you (or their children!) do with the tech you've chosen to use, and struggling to figure it all out can create a lot of additional stress in the home in an already stressful situation. To keep connected and in partnership with caregivers, it's best to offer them and their children some upfront support with a few simple tech tools you'll be using. When everyone feels comfortable with the technology, you'll spend less of your time answering questions about it, and you'll have more time to teach and support students' learning.

How do I do it?

Consider working with colleagues to record a collection of short videos explaining the basics of any tech tools you plan to use with students, or point caregivers and children to short videos that already exist online. Again, it's important to be clear, concise, and explicit, so plan ahead for how you'll present the how-to content.

TIP

In addition to (or instead of) how-to videos, you might create an FAQ document or a shared folder with both password reminders and answers to other technology-related questions.

What are some challenges?

Log-ins, passwords, and websites. Remembering them all. It's a challenge. If there is more than one child in the home, the problem multiples. Here are some options for helping caregivers with this challenge:

- If you are in charge of creating passwords, try to create the same one for every site your students need to access (or suggest students do, if they create their own).
- Teach your students and their caregivers how to save as many passwords to their computer's password manager as possible.
- Suggest caregivers keep a T-chart on the fridge (or other central location) that lists each site's username and password that are in regular use, one chart for each child. These quick, easy references help children problem solve on their own.

VIDEO 2.2
Miss DeMartinis recorded this short video to show her students how to join a Google Meet room. No individual links required!

Hint!

Does your school or district have a designated tech support person? If so, make sure caregivers know how to reach out to that person with technology-related questions so you can remain focused on instruction.

Offer Advice About Setting Up Learning Space(s) at Home

Why is this important?

When children have a dedicated space for "doing school," it can help them separate their work from the rest of their home life in important ways. Caregivers can help children create an environment in this dedicated space that best supports them as learners, or can discuss the few places they might move to or transition to throughout the day as they work.

TIP

In your classroom you probably use lots of visual reminders and scaffolds to support your students as they work, and they can be just as helpful at home. Consider making small, individual anchor charts for children to print out, or invite children to make their own. Make them as visual as possible with lots of pictures or photos that remind students how to do their work independently. You might even take photos of some of the charts in your classroom children use most often and send them to caregivers.

What are some challenges?

Each student's home situation is unique. When you offer advice, it's important to help families consider what's possible given the space they have and the number of other household members who may also need to use the space.

Another challenge is that some children thrive on flexibility and movement and will need the freedom to move within the home as they work rather than staying put at one spot. Regular communication with students and caregivers, and feedback from them about what's working and what's not, can help you tailor your advice.

How do I do it?

To help caregivers think about where children will work, offer general advice that can be helpful in *most* any situation.

- Find space(s) with minimal distractions; it's probably not a good idea to work near a television that's on throughout the day, for example.

Consider This:

Not only do headphones (at home or borrowed from school) help children listen more carefully to class meetings and lessons online, they also can create a quiet "auditory space" where children can focus. Apps or machines that create "white noise" can serve a similar purpose.

- Elicit the child's input about whether a space is working. Ask them, "Can you focus here?" It may take a little trial and error to find the best spot(s).
- If possible, keep organized by placing all the supplies the child needs in one bin or basket, or on one shelf.
- Remember that a dedicated space doesn't have to be a room. It can be the same corner of the kitchen table, or even a lap desk or small three-tiered cart on wheels that is stored away when it's not in use. One middle schooler I know moves his clothes to the far side of his closet and works in there.

Encourage Caregivers to Develop a Schedule and/or Routines

Why is this important?

Most children benefit from routine and consistency (e.g., schoolwork in the morning and play time/TV time in the afternoon). Because this new learning environment requires more independence of children, it's helpful when families create as much consistency across the day as they can. This way, mental real estate is devoted to academic goals, rather than questioning, "When will I eat? Where will I work? What will I do first?" and so on.

How do I do it?

Suggest that families do a quick walk-through of their schedule each day before getting down to business. Talk about any assignment changes, anything the family might be doing that's different, and see if there are any questions.

Depending on the amount of asynchronous instruction you'll be asking children to be involved in (see more on making these choices in Chapters 4 and 6), the age of your students, and/or how much the stress and anxiety of living during a pandemic affects a student's executive function skills, be prepared to give strategies and support for keeping track of schedules. Younger children will likely need more involvement from parents. Older children can learn to manage their work day with strategies such as setting reminders in Google Calendar, making a daily to-do list, or utilizing the "to do" tab in their Learning Management System.

This silent timer doesn't require students to know how to tell time.

DAILY SCHEDULE		
From wake up until 9 a.m.	SOFT START	❑ Make bed. ❑ Make and eat breakfast. ❑ Work on something of your choice.
9:00–9:40	READING	❑ Check in with class, view lesson. ❑ Read for 30 minutes.
9:40–10:20	WRITING	❑ View lesson. ❑ Write for 30 minutes.
10:20–10:30	Dance break!	
10:30–11:10	MATH	❑ View lesson. ❑ Practice problems.
11:10–11:40	Outside time—walk, bike ride, swings	
11:40–12:00	Help make lunch.	
12:00–12:30	Lunch	
12:30–1:30	Free choice	
1:30–2:00	Drawing with Mo Willems	
2:00–3:00	Free-choice screen time (games, shows)	
3:00–5:00	Play outside.	

FROM WAKE UP UNTIL 9 a.m.
❑ Get dressed. ❑ Make your bed. ❑ Eat breakfast. ❑ Brush teeth, brush hair.
9 a.m.–12 p.m.
❑ READ for 30 minutes ❑ WORD study for 15 minutes ❑ WRITE for 30 minutes ❑ MATH for 30 minutes ❑ SCIENCE or SOCIAL STUDIES for 20 minutes
ANYTIME
❑ MOVE (dance, walk, jumping jacks, plank) ❑ HELP (empty dishwasher, fold laundry) ❑ MUSIC (practice your instrument)

These schedules show my family's initial attempt at creating a routine and schedule in our home (above), and the revision after getting feedback from the kids (left). At first, we were overly ambitious with the number of items on the list and too regimented with how we were expecting the children to work. We found that a choice-based routine rather than a minute-by-minute schedule worked better for both our children.

TIP

Visual timers help keep kids on track and focused inside their schedule. Children can set a timer for the entire independent work time, or they can create smaller chunks of time to give themselves breaks. Children get a sense of control from using the timer; it can be empowering while also helping them to self-regulate and self-manage.

What are some challenges?

Although some children will benefit immensely from a clear, consistent schedule, others do better with a "work at your own pace, go in whatever order you want" kind of workflow. Caregivers will need to experiment with scheduling, observe children while working, and ask for their feedback to know what works best. Almost always, however, offering *some* parameters to the day sets kids up for success. The tightness of those parameters depends on the learner.

Consider This:

Choice is a powerful motivator. Encourage caregivers to share control of the daily schedule and offer choices to kids when they are in a rut. "Would you like to begin with math and then come back to writing after you eat lunch?" Or, "Is there another subject you'd like to start with today?" Also consider how your assignments, materials, and the strategies you offer allow for choice as well; know that when you are flexible, it'll be easier for caregivers as well.

Help Families Know What to Do When Things Get Frustrating

Why is this important?

When you spend your days learning alongside kids in classrooms, you know that they sometimes experience frustration or fatigue or even a little defiance in the process. But adults who haven't been in classrooms may *not* know or expect this—especially from their own children! They will almost certainly welcome any advice you can give them for how to deal with it.

How do I do it?

Suggest that families talk through what to do if things get frustrating while a child is working independently (e.g., my password doesn't work, the document closed without saving, I need mom's help but she's busy), and assure them you will teach and practice as much problem solving with their children as you can.

Consider working with the social worker, psychologist, and/or other classroom teachers in your school community to create videos for kids and caregivers to help them coach children through these big feelings. You might also share some self-regulation strategies children (and their caregivers!) can use (see page 33).

TIP

Encourage caregivers to be positive and notice what their children are doing well and to let go if kids seem overwhelmed. Children are living through a pandemic, have had their lives altered, and might have moments when they are unable to work, focus, or attend in the same way they did pre-COVID. Consider sharing the short video titled "Understanding Trauma: Learning Brain vs. Survival Brain" by clinical psychologist, researcher, and professor Dr. Jacob Ham about how brains cannot learn when in survival mode. Children need to be in a calm, safe state to be able to engage with their work (https://drjacobham.com/videos).

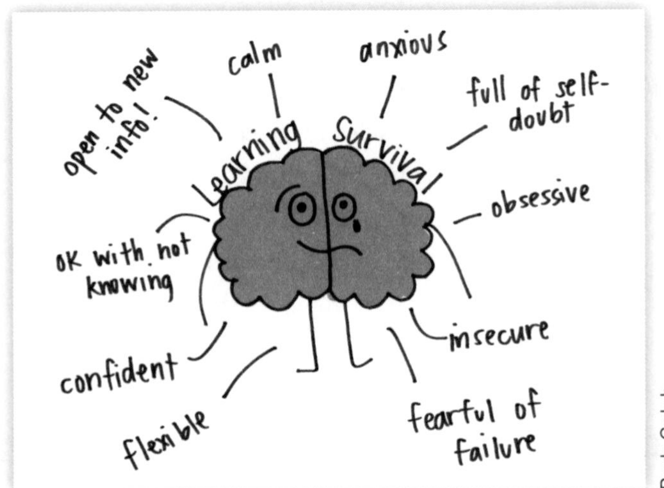

Barb Golub

Visual of the learning brain versus survival brain based on Dr. Ham's talk, "Understanding Trauma"

What are some challenges?

Since homes have morphed into pseudo-classrooms, offices, and twenty-four-hour diners all at once, a few key ground rules can help keep *adults* from becoming frustrated. Ideally, these rules are created with children, rather than dictated to them, and are posted as reminders for everyone. Consider issues such as what qualifies for an interruption in the caregiver's workday, or where to get a snack or a glass of water. Set everyone up for success by addressing these predictable problems and naming ways kids can problem solve and take care of themselves.

Calm Down and Refocus Strategies	
Count to sixty.	Emotions can change in a minute; focusing on the numbers helps give the body a chance to relax and calm.
Smell the flowers, blow out the candles.	Teach this breathing practice where your controlled inhales (through the nose) are the same length as your controlled exhales (through the mouth).
Practice grounding.	Find objects in the room and count up through numbers, grounding yourself in your environment: "I see one refrigerator, two apples, three bananas, four chairs." This also works with colors of the rainbow "I see a red ___, orange ___, yellow ___"; letters "___ starts with A, ___ starts with B . . ."; or senses "I see ___, I smell ___, I feel ___, . . ."
Walk away and move your body.	Leave this open-ended, or post a list of simple exercises to do like three jumping jacks, three side stretches, and a twenty-second plank.
Play with something tactile.	Place focus on an external object that offers sensorial feedback such as modeling clay, a soft or squishy stuffed animal, or kinetic sand.
Do some art.	You might have a corner set up with some colored pencils, crayons, markers, and paper and invite them to visit that area if they need a break from their work.

Chapter 3

Planning and Revising Curriculum Units for Online Instruction

Whether you are teaching in person or online, a well-crafted curriculum is an effective way to ensure you and your students are connected as a learning community, that your teaching is aligned to a clear focus, and that you are all pointed in a common direction.

Clearly communicating what students are expected to do and the ways they can demonstrate their understanding has a powerful positive impact on academic achievement (Fisher, Frey, and Hattie 2016). In curriculum we find a foundation for those expectations; simply put, we have to know what to teach before we can understand what we should expect from learners.

In the online classroom, you are planning instruction with far less time for guided practice, demonstration, and immersion, and expecting students to work more independently. You are teaching in a time when there are endless draws on students' attention. More than ever, student success depends on the extent to which your curriculum is relevant, identity affirming, culturally responsive and sustaining, and doesn't exclude, marginalize, or misrepresent any of your students (Ebarvia 2020; Minor 2018; Souto-Manning et al. 2018; Hammond 2014; España and Herrera 2020). More than ever, you need clearly articulated, streamlined goals focused on the *what* (skills) and *how* (strategies) to smooth the otherwise bumpy path of remote instruction and keep you together with your students, even when you are apart.

Keeping it simple is key, and that's what the strategies in this chapter are all about. Note that the first five strategies are a *sequence* of actions to help you plan or adapt a unit for online instruction and are meant to be read in order.

Step 1: Identify Goals and Skill Progressions

What are goals and skill progressions?

Goal(s) are what you want students to know and be able to do by the end of a unit. You might decide on your focus from your grade-level standards, from noticing student needs, by being guided by the hierarchy of goals for reading and writing (Serravallo 2015, 2017), and/or from reviewing existing curriculum. Perhaps the most engaging and meaningful goals will come from your own students' questions and interests, those that honor and respond to what they most need and want to learn (Casimir 2020).

Skill progressions are pathways of increasing sophistication within a goal. They help you monitor progress, keep you and your students focused, and help students self-assess. You can find skill progressions in standards documents, curricular resources such as Lucy Calkins' Units of Study, or in my books *A Teacher's Guide to Reading Conferences* (2020) or *Understanding Texts & Readers* (2019).

What are some challenges?

When you're teaching in person, you typically plan a unit to last about four to five weeks and include around twenty lessons connected to a few goals. In the remote classroom, it can be more challenging to maintain attention on one overarching unit focus, and you will need to reserve time between lessons for supporting students as they practice independently; this means your units will be shorter (fewer weeks) with fewer lessons connected to only one or two goals. In other words, the unit plans you have used in the past will likely need to be simplified, streamlined, and pared back to what's most essential.

Above and at left are the lists of goals I choose from when designing reading and writing units and/or when articulating literacy goals in content-area studies. All goals are equally important, but they are arranged in a hierarchy of action: those at the top I'd address first, and those at the bottom I'd address later.

How do I do it?

Units can be content focused (e.g., ecosystems), genre focused (e.g., realistic fiction), or offer choice of genre and content and focus on process instead (e.g., independent projects or project-based learning). Once you've figured out your unit focus, follow the Understanding by Design (UBD) model of planning curricular units (Wiggins and McTighe 1998) by first figuring out what you want the end result of the unit to be (goals). Choose from the hierarchy of goals—if your students could benefit from more than one goal, start at the top and work your way down. Take a cue from the Universal Design for Learning (UDL, www.cast.org) and think through any potential barriers students might face in learning these goals and also how you will provide access and challenge for all learners (e.g., support background knowledge, provide graphic representation to concepts, support vocabulary, and so on).

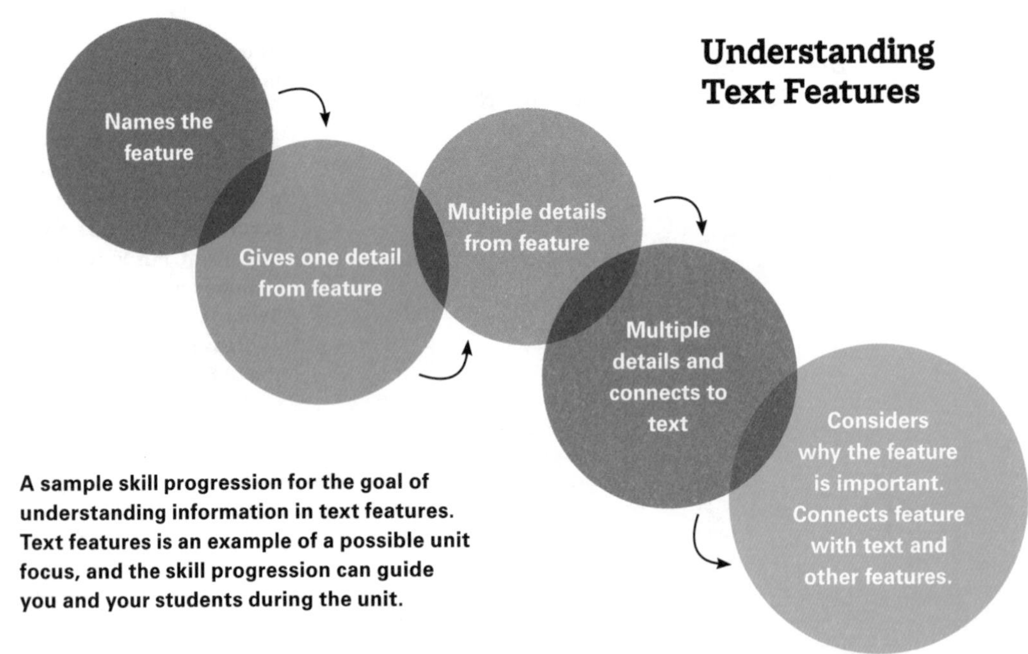

A sample skill progression for the goal of understanding information in text features. Text features is an example of a possible unit focus, and the skill progression can guide you and your students during the unit.

Step 2: Find Anchor Texts

What do you mean by "anchor texts"?

Anchor texts are thoughtfully selected texts that you'll return to again and again while planning and teaching your units. In writing, they are authentic pieces you will use as mentor texts, studying the craft, details, structure, author's inspiration, and more. In reading, they are texts you'll read aloud to your students, discuss together, and refer back to across the unit as you demonstrate strategies.

How do I do it?

For the online classroom, short is best. Think: picture books, poems, short stories, articles. Look for texts that are good examples of the mode and genre the children will be writing or reading and texts that offer plenty of opportunity for them to practice strategies aligned to unit goals. Pay careful attention to who is being represented in the texts you choose, that students see themselves reflected, and that what you choose to focus on causes no harm (Bishop 1990; Jones 2020). Also consider accessibility when selecting texts. For example, choose something that's readily available as a digital text online that you can link to, and/or plan to make a recording of you reading it aloud (www.cast.org).

Suggestion!

Choosing texts that will serve "double duty"—as both a read-aloud text for your reading unit and a mentor text for your writing unit—will save you time and help you streamline your teaching.

TECH NUTS AND BOLTS

- Search whatever e-book database you know all your students have access to—Epic!, Libby, and so on. When the text is already available digitally, you can easily screenshot pages to include in slides and direct children to reread it on their own. Some sites even have a "read to me" feature that provides additional access.
- Using iDocCam or another app like it, turn your phone or tablet into a document camera by connecting it to your computer. If all you have is a hard copy of a text you want to use, record a video of yourself reading it aloud, showing the pages and words as you do.

Step 3: Try Out What You'll Ask Students to Do

What do you mean by "try out"?

Whatever type of writing or reading you'll be asking students to do—write a persuasive letter, read a fantasy novel—write it or read it yourself first. When you do, you can see what parts are challenging and what sorts of strategies you use as a writer or reader, and you will better understand what students might need you to teach them.

How do I do it (for reading)?

Read the text you've selected, pausing often and noticing what you do as a reader, especially the things you do aligned to the goal(s) you'll be teaching in your unit. What are you doing to be able to read it fluently? Understand the character? Visualize the setting? Notice symbolism? Interpret the theme? Flag your book with sticky notes that capture your thinking and ideas, and try to name what you did to make sense as you read. For example, you might note:

- "I got confused in the transition from one scene to the other. I backed up and reread the last page, and then reread this page to make sure the transition between them was clear."
- "The character surprised me here! I compared how she acted (and what words I'd use to describe her) at the start of the story and what she's like now. This helps me say more about her as a character."

Bonus!

When you try something out, save your work, and you've just created your own models and exemplars!

How do I do it (for writing)?

First, study the mentor text you've selected. Notice things such as:

- what the piece is about and how the writer might have gotten an idea for it
- how the piece is organized
- the sorts of details that are included
- word choice and figurative language.

Again, align your noticings to your unit goals as much as you can. Then, try to write in the same genre, paying attention to how you're doing what you're doing. Mark up the margins of your draft with notes about the strategies you used and the decisions you made. You might notice, for example:

- what you did to come up with an idea for the topic
- how you chose to start or end the piece
- when you chose to start new paragraphs
- decisions about punctuation
- choices about words.

Step 4: Design Assessments

Why is this important?

When your teaching needs to be so much leaner and more focused, knowing how students are doing is crucial. When you find out what students already know before the unit begins, and you track and monitor their progress along the way, you can better target your instruction to what they need in the limited time you have. And just like in the classroom, you'll need to identify what they are able to do by unit's end. Not all assessments need to be official, capital A *assessments*. Some can (and should!) be informal and formative.

What are some challenges?

In the classroom, checking in with students verbally, peeking over their shoulder as they work, or handing out and collecting assessments on paper is routine. But in the online classroom, you have to be more strategic and plan carefully for how you will collect information from children. Also, not all children will be able to show you what they know using a single modality; offering options will be crucial to providing universal access (www.cast.org; Minor 2018).

For both reading and writing, you can use skill progressions (see Step 1 on page 36) to evaluate student work before, during, and at the unit's end, but you still have to decide *how* you'll ask students to show you what they know and what options you'll give them for representing their knowledge.

How do I do it (for reading)?

Although there are lots of ways this could go, here a few simple possibilities:

- Choose a short text that you can easily send to students, and/or plan to make a read-aloud video of the text. After reading, ask students to record a video message, fill out a form, or talk to you in a conference about the text. You can evaluate their written or verbal responses using the skill progression(s) aligned to unit goals.
- Using the books they are reading independently, ask students to respond to unit-aligned questions at any point in the unit. It's OK if you haven't read the specific book they are writing about because you're looking at the *quality of response* and not for a specific "right answer." For more on this type of assessment, see *Understanding Texts & Readers*, Part IV (Serravallo 2019).

How do I do it (for writing)?

For writing, prompt children to create a piece on demand before the unit begins. Give options for composing by hand, word processing, or possibly even recording themselves reading aloud what they have written. Save their work. Look at the writing they do throughout the unit, and the piece that they publish (offering again the same modalities) after working through the whole writing process. Use skill progressions to notate progress, give feedback, and set individual goals.

Important!

Make sure to vary your modalities when assessing (i.e., written, verbal) to allow students to best show what they know.

TECH NUTS AND BOLTS

- **Flipgrid:** Invite children to record a message to you in response to a prompt, read aloud to assess their fluency, and so on.
- **E-forms** (e.g., Google Form): Set up a form for easy data collection and view responses from individuals or collect them and notice trends across the class.
- **Shared documents:** Use the comments features in shared documents to give and get feedback from students and to keep an eye on their writing as they work.
- **Conversations:** Whether by phone or videoconference using Zoom or similar, confer with students to assess their understandings and skills (more in Chapter 6).
- **Photos:** Ask students to share a photo of their work by email or app such as Seesaw, or add it to an online shared folder.

Step 5a: Map Out Daily *Reading* Lessons with Goals and Strategies

What do you mean by "map out lessons"?

Once you've made decisions about goals, assessments, and texts, you'll need to figure out the order and flow of your unit and plot out the strategies. Of course, you may need to revise your schedule of lessons as you see how children are responding, but mapping it all out helps you see the overall shape of the unit and stay focused on where you're headed.

How do I do it?

Make a grid to represent the number of weeks you'll spend on the unit. For reading, block out several (three to six) teaching days to focus on one goal, and plan on teaching (or reteaching) multiple strategies over the course of the week or two connected to the goal. A unit ends with a celebration.

Week 1	Understanding Main Idea	Understanding Main Idea	Understanding Main Idea	Flex day for extra support—conferring and small group	Understanding Main Idea
Week 2	Understanding Main Idea	Understanding Main Idea	Identifying Key Details	Identifying Key Details	Flex day for extra support—conferring and small group
Week 3	Identifying Key Details	Main Idea + Details = Summarizing	Main Idea + Details = Summarizing	Main Idea + Details = Summarizing	Celebrate!

Now, go back to your map and insert strategies. If you're using *The Reading Strategies Book*, you'll pull from chapters associated with each goal, paying attention to the level range recommended on the margin of each page (Serravallo 2015). For example, in the following nonfiction unit map, you'll see strategies that begin with an 8 (the chapter on determining main idea) and 9 (the chapter on identifying key details).

Tip

To build enthusiasm and help make your plans clear, you might create a very short video to introduce students and their families to the unit—the main goals, what their work will look like, and what you'll explore together. If not a video, perhaps a short information page. Either document could be emailed to families or housed on your shared space (e.g., class blog or Google Classroom).

Week 1	**Understanding Main Idea** 8.2 Notice What Repeats	**Understanding Main Idea** 8.3 Topic/ Subtopic/ Details	**Understanding Main Idea** 8.7 Paraphrase Chunks, Then Put It Together	**Flex day for extra support—conferring and small group**	**Understanding Main Idea** 8.16 What? and So What?
Week 2	**Understanding Main Idea** 8.8 Sketch in Chunks	**Understanding Main Idea** 8.16 What? and So What? *(reteach)*	**Identifying Key Details** 9.6 Consistently Ask, "How Do I Know?"	**Identifying Key Details** 9.8 Read, Cover, Remember, Retell	**Flex day for extra support—conferring and small group**
Week 3	**Identifying Key Details** 9.13 Important Versus Interesting	**Main Idea + Details = Summarizing** 8.5 Boxes and Bullets	**Main Idea + Details = Summarizing** 8.11 Add up Facts to Determine Main Idea	**Main Idea + Details = Summarizing** 8.19 Consider Structure	**Celebrate!**

Sample unit plan. Numbers and strategy titles refer to lessons in *The Reading Strategies Book* (Serravallo 2015).

Step 5b: Map Out Daily *Writing* Lessons with Process and Strategies

What do you mean by "map out lessons"?

For writing, map out your lessons to support the writing process your students will follow across the unit, and then fill in the strategies you plan to teach each day. Just as with reading, you may need to revise the map as you see how children are responding, and also know that individual children might work at their own pace despite the step of the process you anchor your teaching to each day.

How do I do it?

Make a grid to represent the number of weeks you'll spend on the unit. On the next page is a modified version of a map originally published in *The Writing Strategies Book* (Serravallo 2017). Although that map had twenty lessons, this one for online learning has twelve spots for lessons with flex days built in for reteaching and/or additional conferring and small-group support.

Week 1	Generating and collecting ideas	Generating and collecting ideas	Generating and collecting ideas	Flex day for extra support—conferring and small group	Generating and collecting ideas
Week 2	Choosing an idea to pursue	Flex day for extra support—conferring and small group	Developing the idea	Rehearsing and drafting	Drafting
Week 3	Revising	Flex day for extra support—conferring and small group	Revising	Publishing	Celebrate!

You can dig through professional books and other writing instructional resources to find strategies to teach each day, or craft your own. Keep your lessons focused on your goals for the unit and make sure they also support students as they work through the process you've mapped out. The strategies mapped out in the unit plan on the following page come from *The Writing Strategies Book*. The goals of the unit are generating ideas (strategies come from goal 3 in the book and begin with the number 3 on the chart) and elaboration (strategies beginning with 6), with eight of the twelve lessons connecting back to those goals.

Week 1	**Generating and collecting ideas** 3.1 Important People	**Generating and collecting ideas** 3.2 Moments with Strong Feelings	**Generating and collecting ideas** 3.5 Mapping the Heart	**Flex day for extra support—conferring and small group**	**Generating and collecting ideas** 3.10 Scrapbook Your Life (to Write About It Later)
Week 2	**Choosing an idea to pursue** 4.7 Ask Questions to Focus	**Flex day for extra support—conferring and small group**	**Developing the idea** 5.8 Uh-Oh . . . UH-OH . . . Phew	**Rehearsing and drafting** 6.4 Act It Out . . . Then Get It Down	**Drafting** 6.9 "What *Else* Happened?"
Week 3	**Revising** 6.13 Show, Don't Tell: Using Senses to Describe Places	**Flex day for extra support—conferring and small group**	**Revising** 6.33 How Does Your Character Talk?	**Publishing** 4.4 Write a Title	**Celebrate!**

Sample unit plan. Numbers and strategy titles refer to lessons in *The Writing Strategies Book* (Serravallo 2017).

Streamline and Simplify: Connect Goals *Across* Reading and Writing

What do you mean by "connect goals"?

Reading and writing go hand in hand. When you connect reading and writing goals, every lesson reiterates, duplicates, and reteaches from another angle. In the remote classroom, when the need to keep things streamlined becomes even more critical, connecting goals also helps you make the most of your limited time.

How do I do it?

The chart that follows highlights the natural connections between reading and writing goals as described in *The Reading Strategies Book* and *The Writing Strategies Book* (Serravallo 2015, 2017).

Reading and Writing Connections

Reading	Writing
Reading the Pictures Before children read conventionally, they can learn to storytell from pictures and learn from photos and illustrations in nonfiction texts.	**Composing with Pictures** Before children use letters to write words, they can learn to use pictures to record ideas, storytell, teach, and/or persuade.
Engagement Engaged readers are focused, have stamina to read for long stretches, and choose books that are interesting and important.	**Engagement** Engaged writers take initiative in their own projects, write for sustained periods of time, and find enjoyment in some part of the process (or at least in having written).

continues

Reading and Writing Connections	
Reading	**Writing**
Print Work Print work is (in part) an ability to decode text. Knowing certain rules for how words work and flexibly using strategies to figure out what words say, while also having automaticity with other words, allows students to read with accuracy.	**Spelling** Spelling is (in part) an ability to encode. Knowing certain rules for how language works and having automaticity with the spellings of some words helps students write with accurate, conventional spelling.
Fluency Fluent readers read smoothly, and with expression and intonation.	**Engagement** Engaged writers write with fluency, letting their words flow onto the page without interruption. **Punctuation and Grammar** Writers make choices about punctuation (what to use and where) and construct sentences to communicate how to read a text.
Plot and Setting To comprehend a story, readers need to know how the story is put together, how the events connect, what the problems are, and where the events are taking place.	**Structure and Organization** A story writer considers how the piece will be organized and how much detail to include in each part, so the story flows and is easy to understand. **Elaboration** A story writer considers what details to include and what to leave out to show actions, events, and setting.
Text Features Readers of nonfiction texts need to read the entire page, text *and features*, to comprehend the information the author is teaching.	**Structure and Organization** Writers of informational texts consider how to present the information they want to share—what should be included in the main text, and what should be included in features. **Elaboration** One way writers of informational texts add more information is to add visual features (pictures, illustrations, maps, graphs) that show and explain their facts.
Character Understanding characters—their feelings, traits, actions, and relationships—is an important part of understanding a story.	**Elaboration** Writers bring the characters in their stories to life and help readers understand them when they develop details about their traits, feelings, and actions.

Bonus! *When a student's reading and writing strengths and needs align, or when a strength in one area might support a need in another, you might use the chart to support the student's individual goals during conferences or small groups.*

Reading	Writing
Vocabulary and Figurative Language Readers need to understand the words and phrases the author uses.	**Word Choice** Writers carefully consider and choose words to match their meaning.
Themes and Ideas Readers interpret a story to understand central lessons and messages, symbolism, and social issues.	**Focus** A story writer decides on a focus. For some students the focus will be a point in time (a "small moment"), but for others the focus can be a central idea, theme, message, or issue.
Main Idea When reading informational or persuasive texts, it's important for readers to identify what a text is mostly about and what slant/angle/idea the author has about the topic.	**Focus** Writers of informational or persuasive texts must clarify what their work is mostly about so they can include information that aligns to their intended meaning and doesn't distract readers with extraneous information.
Key Details Readers of informational and persuasive texts need to understand and identify the details that support and connect to the main idea(s) of a text.	**Elaboration** Writers of informational and persuasive texts need to back up their topics and ideas with details such as facts and statistics. **Structure and Organization** Writers of informational and persuasive texts typically use sections and chapters to organize their work by subtopics, and include details that go with those subtopics in those parts.
Conversation Readers benefit from spending time with peers in partnerships and small groups to deepen their understanding about a text, clarify misunderstandings, and engage in social experiences around books. In reading, they need to be taught ways to communicate effectively, and how to listen when a peer is speaking.	**Writing Partners and Clubs** Writers benefit from spending time with peers in partnerships and small groups to generate ideas, test out ideas, get suggestions for revision, edit their work, and more. In writing, they need to be taught ways to communicate effectively, and how to listen when a peer is speaking or sharing their writing.
Writing About Reading To write about reading (to jot to hold on to ideas and develop those ideas in longer entries) connects to many writing goals. To write about reading, a reader needs to generate an idea, have some way to structure the writing, and be sure the writing is focused on one idea. To write longer, the writer needs to elaborate on their thinking with details and support from the text.	

Plan for a Monthly Focus: Genre, Content, Independent Projects, or a Mix

What do you mean by "monthly focus"?

One way to ensure connections between reading and writing is to choose an overarching monthly focus and then tie your unit topics and goals back to that focus. Sometimes the focus might be a mode (e.g., narrative) or genre of writing (e.g., fiction), other times you might choose a content focus (e.g., communities around the world), and still other times you might decide to support students' independent projects and focus your teaching on processes (e.g., working with partnerships and clubs).

How do I do it (mode or genre focus)?

Decide on a genre or mode as your focus (e.g., narrative, information), craft reading and writing unit titles that match the focus, and then plan to teach up to two goals for each unit that connect to that focus.

Mode Focus	Reading Unit and Goals	Writing Unit and Goals
Narrative	**Fiction short stories** *Goal:* Understanding plot and setting *Goal:* Understanding character	**Fiction short stories** *Goal:* Structure *Goal:* Elaboration
Information	**Nonfiction short articles** *Goal:* Determining main idea *Goal:* Identifying key details	**Research-based informational articles** *Goal:* Focus *Goal:* Elaboration

How do I do it (content focus)?

Think about the content area goals (what students will know) and skills (what students will be able to do), and then choose reading and writing goals that best align to what you're studying. Below is one example. Notice the connection of place/setting across the content, reading, and writing goals.

Content Focus	Reading Unit and Goals	Writing Unit and Goals
Communities around the world *Goal:* Explore own identities and the community in which they live *Goal:* Learn how different cultures and customs are unique or similar in four different countries around the world	**Traditional stories (from countries being studied)** *Goal:* Understanding plot and setting *Skills:* Retelling, visualizing setting *Goal:* Understanding themes and ideas *Skills:* Inferring lessons or morals	**Writing stories (set in countries being studied)** *Goal:* Elaboration *Skills:* Developing and describing setting *Goal:* Focus *Skills:* Telling stories with a focus on a lesson or message

TIP

As you plan your units across the year, try to balance modes of writing and consider returning to the same mode later in the year to increase the sophistication of the strategies you teach. For example, if you taught a narrative unit in September and you taught children to focus on a moment, organize a narrative in sequence, and add a few kinds of detail, you might return to narrative later in the year but switch to fiction. In this unit you might teach students how to focus based on a lesson or message, structure a story with rising action, and add more sophisticated details such as showing not telling or using metaphor.

Consider This:

Independent projects work well in classes where students have already developed community, you've figured out ways to meet with children regularly, students are working independently with a sense of agency, and where they have already explored a writing process with you.

How do I do it (independent projects)?

With independent projects, students choose a topic to explore, something they want to make, or a problem to solve, and then they read and write in connection to what they are exploring. As Dena Simmons (2020) recommends, "As we come up with remote-learning lessons, let's consider employing projects that rely on what families have at their disposal (resources and capabilities), and invite students to select topics that are not only relevant and interesting to them, but also tied to devising solutions to their current realities."

With independent projects, you will plan for more process-focused curriculum: research skills, project management skills, working collaboratively with partners and club, and so on. See the following example.

Process Focus	Reading Unit and Goals	Writing Unit and Goals
Conversation and Collaboration	**Book Clubs (Fiction Genre Choice)** *Goal:* Improving conversation *Goal:* Understanding character	**Independent Projects with the Support of Friends** *Goal:* Partners and clubs

Bonus!

Check out the free launching units designed by the brilliant Kristi Mraz, available on her website (http://bit.ly/2Quxbwl). They are designed specifically for this time, though they'd work well post-pandemic too, with community building, identity, agency, relationships, and support at their center.

A student's independent project may focus on a content study or be framed by a problem that needs to be solved (e.g., engaging more voters, reducing greenhouse gases, eliminating plastic ocean pollution). In this case, your literacy goals, skills, and strategies may be chosen in response to what you see in their work.

Project Focus: Marine Biology	Student Goal(s) and Skill(s)
During reading, the student studies a variety of books about sea turtles, noting along the way how problems such as poaching, entanglement in fishing nets, and habitat destruction are threatening the species, along with a list of possible solutions to the problems.	Your conferring focuses on helping them read the articles they select carefully, with strategies for determining main idea and key details.
During writing, the student drafts a persuasive article to inform readers about what they discovered in their studies and includes a list of options for possible action to help save the species.	Your conferring helps them to articulate their thesis and provide the key details (elaboration) that best make their points.

One example of a student's self-selected independent study project and the literacy goals and skills to support their work.

How do I do it (blending all options)?

If you employ all three options, rotated throughout the year, your planning may look something like the following example.

September	Reading	Writing
Reading/writing focused *Overarching Ideas:* Identity, community-building, building engagement in reading and writing	*Unit:* **Reading Stories** *Goal:* Engagement *Skills:* Reflecting on self as readers, personal reading histories *Goal:* Understanding plot and setting *Skills:* Visualizing, retelling, inferring from details	*Unit:* **Personal Narrative** *Goal:* Engagement *Skills:* Generating meaningful topics, sustaining writing for longer stretches, reflecting on writing histories *Goal:* Elaboration *Skills:* Slowing down action and adding elaboration
October	**Reading**	**Writing**
Content focused *Unit:* Exploring Ecosystems in Our Backyards, Parks, and Sidewalks *Goals:* Living and nonliving components of an ecosystem Key factors that impact life in an ecosystem Interactions among organisms that affect stability	*Unit:* **Nonfiction** *Goal:* Determining main idea *Goal:* Identifying key detail	*Unit:* **Nonfiction** *Goal:* Structure *Goal:* Focus
November	**Reading**	**Writing**
Independent project focused *Unit:* Explore a Problem, Propose a Solution	*Skills:* Conversation and collaboration with peers *Skill:* Engagement *Goal:* TBD, based on individual needs and genre choices from each reader	*Goal:* Generating ideas *Skills:* Generating meaningful topics, adapting topics, exploring genres *Skills:* Selecting and studying mentor texts *Goal:* TBD, based on individual needs and genre choices from each writer

Organize Your Curriculum and Resources in a Learning Management System

What is a Learning Management System?

A Learning Management System (LMS; sometimes called Learning Management *Platform*) allows you to organize, manage, and share content—from lessons to shared texts to assessments and more. An LMS helps you build a digital learning environment and may include tools for recording, polling, surveying, collecting information through forms, videoconferencing, and storing and organizing resources such as skill progressions, rubric, charts, organizers, and more.

How do I do it?

The first step is to choose which platform you'll use. Some of those available are free, although others are a bit pricey. Some require less up-front training and are quite intuitive, but others require a bit of a learning curve. In many cases, the decision might be made for you as your school or district has chosen and licensed one consistent platform for all teachers to use. If not, one of the free options (e.g., Google Classroom) may be your best bet.

Once you have your system or platform, you'll need to learn how to use it. If your district or school chose a system for you, hopefully they will provide some professional learning to help you get comfortable.

VIDEO 3.1
Watch Ms. DeMartinis' video about how to find comments in Google.

If not, look for freely available videos online to walk you through setting up and managing your online classroom. Start with:

- learning how to connect with children and families (videoconferencing, email, instant messaging)
- learning how to post videos/lessons
- learning how to post assignments and receive completed assignments back from students
- figuring out how to organize and store reference materials.

TIP

Remember, just as you'll need to learn how to navigate this system as a teacher (posting, organizing, etc.), your students and families will need to learn how to find what they need, turn things in, and communicate with you. Share short video tutorials that you create or that are available online.

TECH NUTS AND BOLTS

I'm not endorsing any of these LMSs over another; they are simply examples of what's available.

- Google Classroom
- Canvas
- Schoology
- Microsoft Teams

Approach Your Planning and Teaching with Flexibility and Feedback

What do you mean by "flexibility and feedback"?

You'll plan weeks (or sometimes months) of curriculum at a time. To plan, you'll make assumptions about your students as learners and about their existing skills and needs. Once you get into a unit, it's important to monitor students' engagement and progress, invite feedback from your learners, and be flexible to adjust (adding lessons in, taking lessons out, changing the pace, and so on) as you teach.

What are some challenges?

When you're live and in person with children, you can easily gauge their level of energy, how much they're "with" you, how excited (or bored) they are, and adapt accordingly. When you're teaching online, and especially when you're offering recorded lessons, it can be harder to determine how students are responding.

How do I do it?

Invite students to give you feedback by having them fill out a form or quick survey (Google Forms, SurveyMonkey), polling them at the start of a lesson with a tool such as Mentimeter, or asking them to send you an email with some feedback midunit.

Raffaella De Martinis
Apr 3

Nice job reaching the end of Week Three! If you need to finish work over the weekend, you definitely can. Please make sure you check over each slide and click "turn in."

Please comment below how week three went for you.
What did you like? What was challenging?
How did you enjoy the Google Slides?
How did you like the videos?
What story was your favorite?

I would love to hear your feedback!

6 class comments

Tessa Apr 3
I liked on google sides we were able to see when we should stop working. I liked the videos because they helped us now what to do. I liked all the stories so I don't really have a favorite story.

Niko Apr 3
I liked science and writing. I LOVED SLIDES, because it was easier and more fun than before. I also liked the videos because they told us what we had to do. I thought that finding where we had to continue the next day was kinda challenging. I enjoyed all of the stories but my favorite one was " Those Darn Squirrels"!

Raffaella De Martinis Apr 3
Thank you for the feedback! I love the stories too.

Raffaella De Martinis Apr 3
I am so glad you liked the slides! That is a really funny story. I hope you are able to find the next day's slides a little bit better now.

Shekinah Apr 5
I like the videos

Finn Apr 6
I liked the slides.

Ms. DeMartinis asked her students to respond within Google Classroom about how the week's lessons went and which formats (video, slide, story) they enjoyed.

Even without eliciting feedback, you might be able to tell some things about engagement by students' responses to assignments. For example, if lots of students don't log on or complete assignments, especially when they have in prior units, you might suspect that things are dragging and it's time to move on. Also ask students about whether the pace of the unit is too fast or too slow, if they need more catch-up days, or if there's any confusion and they need more small-group guided practice along the way (see Chapter 6 for help with that).

TECH NUTS AND BOLTS

- **Google Forms or SurveyMonkey:** Create a simple form with various question types (short or long responses, multiple choice, choose all that apply, Likert scale, etc.). View answers from individuals or look at class trends.
- **Mentimeter:** Create a poll and generate a quick link that can be embedded into a slideshow and used during live instruction. Students can view results in real time.

Chapter

4

Managing Your Time Across a Day, Across the Week

At the beginning of remote instruction last spring, it was common to hear stories of overwhelmed teachers spending fourteen- to sixteen-hour days managing it all, risking burnout. Of *students* who didn't log in for anything, and just disappeared. Of *parents*, overwhelmed with trying to balance their job responsibilities—or dealing with losing their jobs—all while supporting students' learning at home. None of us signed up for this. We are in the middle of a pandemic. People are getting sick and dying. It *is* all overwhelming.

That said, for many children, structure brings comfort. For many adults, having their children meaningfully engaged brings a sense of calm and normalcy. Connection to other people, especially during a time of forced distancing, can bring joy. Learning releases endorphins. Schoolwork can also serve as a helpful distraction and give children something to focus on.

I think one solution is to manage expectations—for yourself, for families supporting kids at home (or those who can't), for your students. You don't need to run your online classroom as you would an in-person classroom. Instead, try to focus (and in some cases reduce) goals for your curriculum (see Chapter 3), focus goals for students, maximize the time you do have, and set limits.

The strategies in this chapter and the next (Chapter 5) are all meant to help you think about how you and your students spend your time each day. We'll start with your time, and the goal is for you to create a weekly schedule that allows you to do good work and focus on things that matter, all while taking care of yourself and your family. As you consider these possibilities, I recommend keeping your work day to six hours all-in—including planning, collaborating, recording lessons, giving feedback, conferring, and working with small groups. After you read about your time and your students' time, Chapter 6 zooms in (pun intended) and shows you how to move the methods and lesson types you use in the classroom to an online space.

I offer these strategies knowing that every community has its own unique set of challenges (from availability of devices, Wi-Fi, and books; to the school or district's plan for online-only or hybrid approach; to the number of community members impacted by the virus, and more). In some places, districts and unions will be dictating what can and must happen, and in other places, teachers might be left to figure it out on their own—which can be freeing, but also overwhelming.

Excellent teaching and support look different for every learner, and what will be right for each teacher will be different, too. I hope the strategies that follow help you find balance, while staying true to your priorities.

Understand the Pros and Cons of Synchronous and Asynchronous Teaching

What is synchronous teaching?

Synchronous instruction is what you do in your normal classroom—you teach at the same time students are learning: *live*. Being online with your students at the same time, working together, will feel most like "normal life," and this time is essential for guided practice, coaching students as they apply strategies across contexts, supporting and monitoring independent practice, and having opportunities to meaningfully connect. Synchronous teaching can provide socially isolated children a sense of community (Flaherty 2020). An added bonus of going live with children in their homes is that caregivers can benefit from seeing how you work with their children; invite them to sit alongside their child and they can use some of your same teaching moves to coach their children in between your meetings with them.

What is asynchronous teaching?

With asynchronous teaching, you'll record lessons at times that work best for you, and students can participate at a time convenient to them and their families. They can also rewind and participate in lessons many times over.

What are some challenges with synchronous and asynchronous teaching?

It may feel most natural to try and translate everything you did in the classroom into the virtual world synchronously, but it may be challenging to do for a variety of reasons. If you teach multiple sections of the same

Consider This:

*Notice the advice in this strategy is to **teach** whether you're doing it live or in a recording. Links to worksheets, or slide decks with assignments but no strategies are less effective than recorded lessons. Placing a camera in a classroom to livestream the happenings without any interaction between the teacher and the at-home students is less effective than guided practice.*

class, which also means kids have multiple teachers, scheduling can be a challenge. If you work with families who share a device (an access and equity challenge), your students may need to work during "off-hours" because of other commitments. And then there's just the fact that being on Zoom (or other videoconference platforms) all day can be physically and emotionally draining (Blum 2020).

With asynchronous teaching, you lose the interaction and immediacy of feedback that's possible with live teaching, so you'll need to plan ways to make the recordings engaging and interactive, invite response and practice, and collect feedback and assessment information (see Chapter 6).

How do I do it?

You'll need to be *flexible* and aim for a *balance* of asynchronous and synchronous instruction, knowing that it does not need to be the same way every day, or even the same for every student (Reich 2020a, 2020b; Greenberg 2020; Rappolt-Schlichtmann 2020). See pages 78–81 for an overview of how both might fit into a daily schedule.

Invite Your Students Online with You for Some Time Each Day

Why is this important?

Feedback from the spring showed that classes that engaged in a regular morning meeting/community circle time engaged with their day's work with more consistency and regularity than those who did not (Center for Collaborative Classroom 2020). It can also support students socially and emotionally and help reduce isolation (Rappolt-Schlichtmann 2020; Flaherty 2020).

Consider This:

Depending on the age of your students, you might find rotating smaller groups are a better option than whole-class meetings.

How much time do I need?

Whole-class meetings can be brief (think fifteen minutes to half an hour) and can be used for conversation, celebrations, games, and/or to support academic goals such as a whole-group read-aloud and conversation or whole-group writing mentor text study. However you decide to use the time, remember that the key is *connection*, bringing your students together as part of a community.

What are some challenges?

Not all students who are invited will log in—some because they don't want to, and some because they can't. Live/synchronous options (e.g., "Join via this link at this time") can be challenging when students work with multiple teachers, when there are multiple children in the home, and/or when devices are scarce. Be flexible and understanding, and make sure you record the meeting and save it somewhere for those who aren't able to join.

Plan and Record Short Whole-Class Microlessons

Why is this important?

Lesson planning is just as important when you're teaching online as it is in your classroom, and maybe even more so. Because you are teaching in much shorter segments of time (read more on this in Chapter 6), you need to know exactly what you want to happen in the lesson—no room for sidebars and tangents! Keeping your whole-class recorded lessons short allows more time for flexible, differentiated, small-group and one-on-one teaching.

How much time do I need?

You'll need to set aside about an hour per day or less for lesson preparation and recording. You'll need all of this time if you're creating lessons for all of the core subject areas as a self-contained elementary teacher (aim for one microlesson each day for reading, writing, and math, plus a read-aloud), and less time if you teach multiple sections of the same class, and the same recording can be shared with multiple sections. Each lesson should be short, around three minutes long (more on this topic in Chapter 6). If you are also responsible for teaching content area studies (more on this in Chapter 5), you may need another hour per week on average to record science and social studies lessons or post activities or texts for students to engage with.

How do I do it?

Start by reviewing student work and your notes from the prior week to see what students most need. Then, prepare materials—for example, select a shared text for students to read, create a demonstration text or chart, plan a read-aloud—teach and record the lessons, and then post or upload them to whatever LMS, blog, or platform you're using. If you're planning to teach these short lessons live, you might spend about half this time preparing your lessons, and the balance of that time teaching them live with students (more on this in Chapter 6).

What are some challenges?

Although grade-level teams might be tempted to share the responsibility of recording lessons (one teacher does all the math, one does all the reading, and one does all the writing), this can lead to less authenticity and responsiveness. Also, you may find children are less engaged with learning from teachers they are not as connected to. Instead, you might plan collaboratively with colleagues to come up with demonstration texts and figure out what strategies you're teaching, but each teacher records the lesson for their own class. If you can keep your lessons simple and short, you will find it's not too burdensome.

Host "Office Hours" for Student- and Caregiver-Initiated Response Time

Why is this important?

I'm sure you know that answering emails and texts at all hours of the day and evening is neither practical nor healthy. However, as students are working at home, they have questions, they make connections they want to share, they come to new insights. You can do some of your best, most responsive teaching if they (and their caregivers) have a way to reach out to you about their learning when they are working (Hoffman, Brackett, and Levy 2020). Scheduling a designated time makes it doable and predictable for all.

How much time do I need?

I recommend you set aside one to two hours per day for office hours when students and/or their caregivers might ask questions, connect with you, check in about assignments, and more.

How do I do it?

Make sure the purpose and the schedule for your office hours are clear, and that students and their caregivers know how to contact you—through a consistent videoconference link, a messenger or texting app, or email.

Office Hours Tips

If students are primarily reaching out to you by email or text, you might find it easier and more efficient to talk than text. Consider asking students to ***join you for a quick videoconference***, or even record and send very short videos that teach a strategy or give an example for them to watch when they are able.

For children without Wi-Fi, tablets, or laptops, you might ***connect by phone***.

The more you're able to teach families and children about the tech tools and ***organize FAQs and other resources***, the more you'll be able to spend this time supporting student goals and learning processes.

If you find you have free time during your office hours, you can use it to check in with students' work and ***provide written feedback***.

Consider This:

Assuming each child (or adult helper) seeking support might spend ten to fifteen minutes with you, you could provide personal support for four to eight students and/or families during office hours each day.

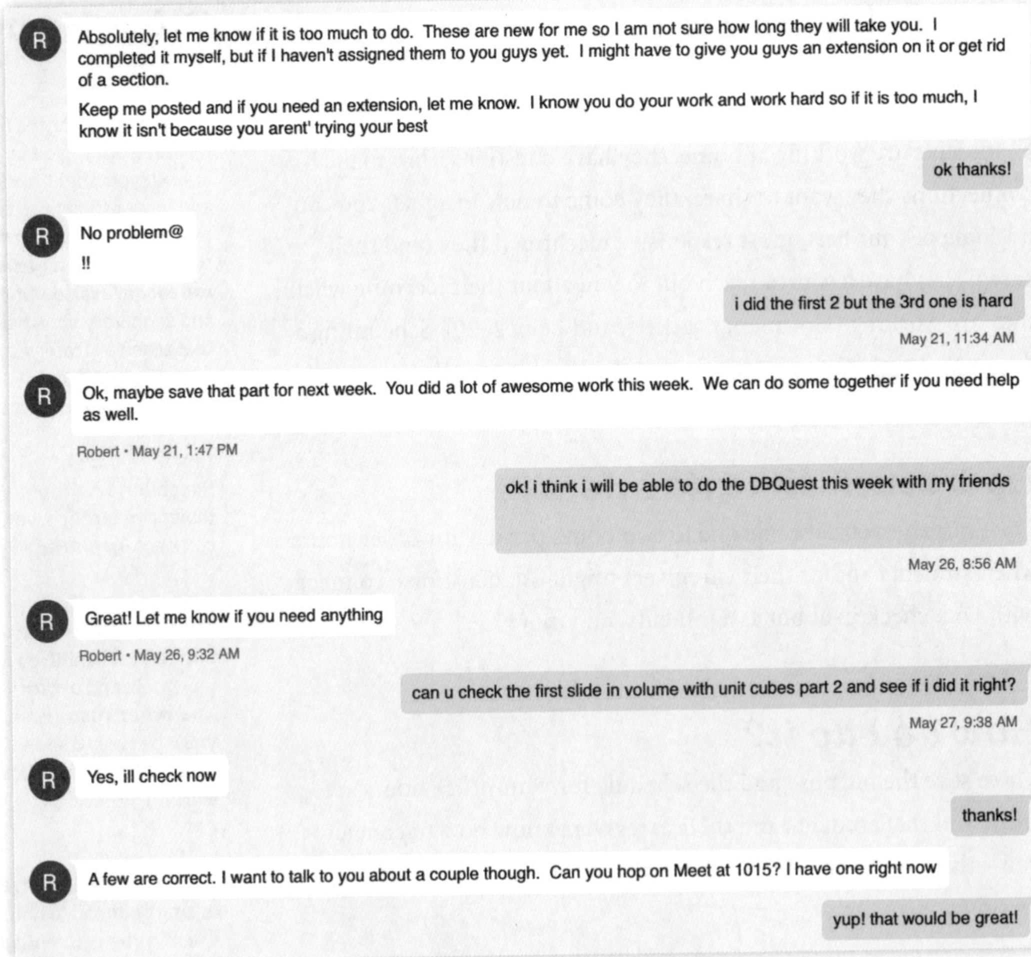

This math teacher opens up his messenger app during office hours and invites questions. He will hop on a video call with a student if a demonstration is warranted or provide written feedback through texts.

Make a Schedule for Conferences and Small Groups

Why is this important?

You may have done a lot of small-group and individual instruction (conferring) before you moved to remote teaching, but even if you didn't, you probably learned pretty quickly that you *need* to work with students in smaller groups when you're teaching online. A computer screen just doesn't offer you the same kind of proximity you need to be responsive to twenty-plus children at once.

How much time do I need?

I recommend you do most of your synchronous teaching in small groups and conferences, so I suggest you set aside two to three hours per day for it. Teachers who teach the same subject to multiple sections will probably find they'll be able to devote more time to working with individuals and small groups each day as they'll need less time for lesson preparation and recording.

How do I do it?

In Chapter 6, you'll learn strategies for working with individuals and small groups of students in an online environment, but first you'll need to play with ways to make the schedule manageable. Here are some options. You might:

- Send out a sign-up once a week and invite children to sign up for the groups they want to participate in in the week ahead (each group might have a different lesson focus and kids can choose what they need). You could use Calendy, an editable Google Doc, or a SignUpGenius sheet to help manage your calendar and available timeslots within.

TIP

In the spring, many teachers commented with frustration that they spent an inordinate amount of time providing written feedback and comments on student work, only to have it ignored. It can be very challenging for students, especially young students, to translate written feedback into action. You may find that if you meet with students regularly in conferences and small groups, you don't need to do so much written feedback. If connecting with children online synchronously is challenging, you might use this time for written feedback and couple what you write with short recorded video lessons showing *how* to do what your feedback suggests.

- Set up consistent meeting times for each student (e.g., Jamal always meets with you on Tuesdays from 10:00 to 10:15 and with his book club and you on Friday from 10:00 to 10:15) and then spend the time reviewing the student's work and focusing on what the student needs most in those moments.
- Block off certain days of the week for certain subjects (e.g., Mondays and Tuesdays are literacy days, Wednesdays and Thursdays are Math, and Friday is catch-up).
- Decide to meet each individual for a longer period of time once a week and cover all subjects during that time (e.g., Isabel meets with you on Wednesdays from 10:00 to 10:40 and you give feedback, demonstrate new strategies, and provide guided practice for her work in math, reading, and writing).

Suggestion!

As you tinker with a schedule for synchronous instruction, keep connection in mind: if you are an elementary teacher, ideally every child will engage with you in a few short conferences and/or small groups each week or one longer individualized session that covers multiple subjects. If you are a teacher in middle school, ideally children will meet with each teacher at least once every 5–7 school days.

What are some challenges?

What will work best for you is based on many factors—your own schedule, your students' schedules, the number of students you have in your class(es), and more. Consider these options, try one for a few weeks, and change if it doesn't seem to be working. Ask students and caregivers for feedback about what's working and not working from their end, too.

Week 10: Check In Chats

Step 1: Go to meet.google.com
Step 2: Click Join
Step 3: Type in:

Thursday	10:15	- Miles - Chiara - attended - Lucas - Angelina - attended
Thursday	10:30	- Jack D. - attended - Trevor - attended - Payton - attended - Brian - Barack
Friday	10:15	- Finn - attended - Shekinah - attended - Chloe - Jack J. - attended
Friday	10:30	- Shea - attended - Marcus - attended - Evie - attended - Tessa - attended - Niko - attended - Ben - attended - Ryan - attended - Shira - attended

A third-grade teacher posts a weekly sign-up sheet using an editable Google Doc to invite students to join when their schedule allows. She keeps track of who showed up in the same shared document. She uses one link for all students and keeps those who log on early in a "waiting room" while she works with her scheduled students.

Preserve Space for Professional Learning and Collaboration

Why is this important?

Taking good care of yourself as a professional is just as important when you are teaching online as it is when you are in your classroom. Collaboration with colleagues is an important way to feel connected and be part of your school community. Whatever your situation, don't leave your own learning to chance. Make a space for it on your schedule.

How much time do I need?

I recommend two to three hours per week.

How do I do it?

Hopefully your school or district is supporting your ongoing professional learning around online instruction, and research-based pedagogy in general. Perhaps you have a literacy or instructional coach who is leading grade-level meetings. Perhaps you are given funds to attend a virtual workshop or conference. In the absence of school- or district-supported professional learning, in the time you carve out you could get together online with colleagues in your grade level to plan, troubleshoot, or share. You might collaborate with other service providers (special educators, the occupational therapist, the physical therapist, the speech and language pathologist) whose input will help shape your plans for students. Maybe your library media specialist has been playing around with a new online tool and wants to share how to use it. You could attend one of the many free webinars being offered by educational publishing companies, read blogs, listen to podcasts, or study professional books like this one.

What are some challenges?

When there is so much new to learn, as there has been in this move to online instruction, it's easy to take on too much and try to learn too many new things at once. Just as you want to focus on one or two goals at a time for your students and you don't expect them to be perfect at everything the first go-round, extend the same patience and grace to yourself.

Map Out a Weekly Schedule and Set Boundaries

Why is this important?

Having a written schedule for each week, printed out and posted by the computer or device where you do your teaching, is a critical part of your own self-care. Consider the schedule to be a set of boundaries meant to protect you, and then hold yourself to them. That's how you can be there for your students *next* week—when you can make adjustments if you need them.

How do I do it?

The different ways of spending time are like moveable pieces of furniture. Think about your own best ways of working and what you know about what best serves your students, and then place them inside a schedule that makes the most sense. Share the times you're available with families, and then be sure to post an auto-generated response when you're *not* available. See the following page for one example of a weekly schedule.

	MONDAY	TUESDAY	WEDNESDAY	THURSDAY	FRIDAY
8:30–9:00	Small-group morning meeting *or* Small-group read-aloud				
9:00–11:00	Individual conferences for reading, writing, and math *or* Small-group lessons 30 minutes each				
	Aubrey Ben Camden Chloe	Cece Earl Evan Hadley	Hailey Isaac Jake Josie	Joey Lily Lucas Natalie	Owen Rhea Saoirse TJ
11:00–11:15	BREAK				
11:15–12:00	Recording lessons for following day (minilessons and read-alouds)				
12:00–1:00	LUNCH				
1:00–2:00	Professional learning	Office hours	Professional learning	Office hours	Professional learning
2:00–3:00	Office hours		Office hours		Office hours

Sample teacher schedule, Ms. Maurantonio (grade 1, twenty students)

	MONDAY	TUESDAY	WEDNESDAY	THURSDAY	FRIDAY
9:00–9:30	Open 30-minute office hours to answer questions about the day's work				
9:30–10:50	Small-group lessons (strategy lessons, book clubs, writing clubs) by sign-up, 20 minutes per lesson, 60 students per week				
	9:30–9:50: book clubs				
	4 students—Book Club A	4 students—Book Club B	4 students—Book Club C	4 students—Book Club D	4 students—Book Club E
	10:00–10:20: strategy lessons—writing				
	4 students	4 students	4 students	4 students	4 students
	10:30–10:50: strategy lessons—reading				
	4 students	4 students	4 students	4 students	4 students
10:50–11:00	BREAK				
11:00–12:00	Office hours and written feedback				
12:00–1:00	Recording lessons, planning, and/or professional learning				
1:00–5:00	BREAK				
5:00–6:00	Office hours and written feedback				

Sample grade 5 ELA teacher schedule (two classes, fifty-two students total). Notice that this teacher schedules an hour in evenings for office hours when families are available and takes a long midday break. (Note: students are expected to be available for synchronous instruction with the ELA teacher from 9:30–11 and with the STEM teacher from 11–12:30.)

Consider This:

The key is, plan to spend ***most*** *of your time during the week in differentiated instruction, in whatever ways work for you and your students. The time recommendations in this chapter are simply meant as suggestions; the balance is up to you.*

What are some challenges?

Depending on the age of your students, when they are doing their work, what other responsibilities they may have, the level of involvement of caregivers as partners, etc., you may find that one format for teaching works better than others. If you do, it makes sense to shift the balance of how you spend your time. For example, if synchronous planned lessons are challenging because you serve families with many children in the home who all need to use the same device, then longer office hours where students can reach out when they have access might work better. Or if you're a middle school teacher with 100+ students who are each working with multiple teachers, scheduling synchronous learning in conferences and small groups might be a real challenge. If so, plan for more impromptu meetings during office hours as students need them.

Another challenge is whether you have your own children at home doing virtual learning, very young children who require attention, or elderly family members you are looking after, all while you are also trying to support your students. Hopefully your school or district will support you in creating a schedule that works for both you and your family as well as the children and families you serve.

Chapter 5

Supporting Students' Independent Practice at Home

When you think about how students should spend their time each day during remote instruction, a key guiding principle is the same whether you're teaching in-person or online: to get better at any skill, learners need time to engage in meaningful repeated practice (Diamond and Lee 2011; Therrien 2004). Across the day in different content areas, many teachers use a workshop model: with this model, a short lesson flows into work time with conferring and small-group instruction for guided practice, and then segues into collaborative time for partners and clubs, and then wraps up with a short time for sharing and reflection.

You can easily modify the workshop model for the online environment, and this is especially true if your students are already familiar with its structures and routines. In fact, one of the benefits of remote instruction, if you're teaching asynchronously at least some of the time, is that students may work independently at their own pace and in whatever order they prefer, so these typical parts of the workshop may not happen sequentially.

In the in-person classroom, a whole-class lesson flows into a long period of independent work with conferring, partner/club time, and small-group instruction, and wraps up with a whole-class share. You could use this structure online and run a fully synchronous workshop (see pages 126–129).

In the online environment, you might invite children to watch a prerecorded lesson, confer with them one-on-one, or work with them in a small group. They will have expectations for independent practice, but lessons they view or participate in may or may not occur directly before their practice time.

Notice that the majority of time, whether in class or online, is devoted to independent practice. Consider that students will need anywhere from twenty to forty minutes of independent practice a day, per subject area or discipline, and that a total remote school day should include about two to three hours of learning/work time (with breaks throughout and potential additional time and support for kids with Individualized Education Programs, 504 Plans, or those who work with an English as a second language teacher).

In the classroom, of course, you keep track of time. When kids are working from home, they might need a timer to make sure they practice for the minimum number of minutes recommended. As mentioned in Chapters 1 and 2, remember that individual students may respond very differently to working from home: for some, the flexibility, the ability to self-direct their work environment and pace themselves will lead to an *increase* in productivity and success with accomplishing their goals. For other students, you and their caregivers may need to provide clear support with making plans and schedules, offering feedback along the way.

Four critical questions about students' work time

1. Do students have a reliable device and Wi-Fi to connect to you and their peers?
2. Is the independent practice students need best done on-screen or off?
3. Do students have the materials they need to be successful in their independent practice?
4. If not, how can you make sure they get what they need?

Ask Students to Read Every Day

How much time do they need?

I recommend you ask students to spend twenty to thirty minutes per day, depending on their age and stamina, plus time to view any recorded lessons or participate in any live lessons or book conversations.

How do I support them?

In the classroom, you typically plan for all the components of the reading workshop to fit into a single class period, but with remote learning, the structure is more flexible. Here are some possibilities for how students might be supported to read with intention each day:

- Students might start by watching a recorded video of a reading minilesson or a read-aloud with strategy instruction that you've posted to your online platform, and then move to independent reading.
- As students read, you might ask them to practice the strategy you taught in the recorded video or read-aloud and/or the strategies they are working on as part of their individual goal.
- Some days, if you're planning to meet with students in conferences or small groups, you might skip the minilesson or read-aloud altogether. Invite students to remind themselves of their individual goals and get right to their reading, and then coach them when you meet with them in a conference, small group, or book club.

- Depending on their age, you might ask students to do some minimal jotting as they read, record their thoughts on paper or a sticky note, and then take a photo and upload their work to share with you or other students. They can also do this in an on-screen form that you've set up or in a shared document. If uploading images of their jottings becomes too burdensome or access to devices is too challenging, students can simply hold onto their notes and share them with you during a check-in, office hours, or a conference or small-group lesson.
- For younger students, some days you might have asynchronous or synchronous phonics, phonemic awareness, or vocabulary lessons and teach them to transfer and apply what they learned to their independent reading.
- Students might meet once or twice a week in partnerships or book clubs to talk with peers about the books they are reading, read together (younger students), or share updates on their strategy work. You may need to be present for these meetings at first, but eventually older students or children with more involved caregivers may be able to set them up and meet on their own.

What are some challenges?

With so much digital content available, it's easy to think that students will have what they need for independent reading practice as long as they have a device and Wi-Fi. But there are student and text variables to consider when making sure children are set up with the materials that are *most* helpful to keep them engaged and practicing the skills and strategies they are focused on with their goals, and that support their comprehension (Serravallo 2019). The key is to ensure that every student has what they need to be successful, and for you to be flexible and nimble with supporting student work at home.

The next four strategies offer suggestions for helping children to get access to books and texts, and for adapting instruction and strategies when students read e-books or listen to audiobooks or podcasts.

Give Students Access to Paper Books

What are some challenges?

We might as well just start right here! Many would agree that nothing beats real paper books when it comes to engagement or comprehension (Wolf 2018, 2020). For many of us, our books were locked away in classrooms when schools closed, and even if you have been able to access them, that still leaves the challenging question, "How do I get books into students' hands?"

How do I do it?

The good news is that schools around the country have been figuring out ways to meet this challenge since the spring of 2020, and maybe one or more of these ideas will work for you and your school community:

Baggies by Bus: In Mattituck-Cutchogue Union Free School District, New York, coaches, librarians, parent volunteers or school aides make book baggies on Monday; the bags go home on the bus route that afternoon, then they're collected on Friday. They sit in the building over the weekend. New books are added to the baggies. Note that current research suggests that COVID-19 can survive on the interior pages of books for up to four days, so it may be wise to keep them "quarantined" longer if possible (Institute of Museum and Library Services 2020).

Deliveries: School staff can deliver books to children's homes. Alternatively, teachers can bring books and materials to students and do a quick, socially distanced conference while they're there.

Books & Meals: Books (from the school library or classroom libraries) are displayed during meal pickups and students create their own book bags for the week. Or, book baggies can be preassembled and families pick them up when they get their meal or pantry items (Spaulding 2020).

Bonus!

Check out Molly Ness' podcast End Book Deserts *for more practical ideas and inspiration (http://bit.ly/34PQGaU).*

Public Libraries: Local libraries have created book baggies that are available for curbside pick-up or even deliverable by drone (O'Kane 2020)!

Swap & Share: If you live in a community where families can afford to purchase books, consider matchmaking kids in the same class or grade level who have similar tastes in books. Families can trade books to help each purchase go the extra mile. In some communities, Facebook Swap groups help match up "in search of" with "who needs a" posts.

Book Drives: In Northport, Long Island, Molly Feeney Wood organized a new book drive by partnering with her local independent bookstore, Book Revue. Books were purchased by families for their own use and a portion of each sale went to buy new books. Purchasers could also buy a book to donate. They were then distributed at a food pantry in Northport High School.

Partner with Local Organizations: Across the country, different organizations have spearheaded efforts to get books into the hands of students, particularly those for whom access is a challenge. Here are a few to check out and be inspired by:

- Start Lighthouse, based in the South Bronx: startlighthouse.org
- Bernie's Book Bank, based in Chicago: berniesbookbank.org
- The Conscious Connect, based in Springfield, Ohio: theconsciousconnect.org
- Gaining Ground, based in Broken Arrow, Oklahoma: gaininggroundliteracy.org.

Little Free Libraries: Some teachers have mapped out the Little Free Libraries in their town and shared the location of these pickup/dropoff spots with families.

Drop Off Donations: In South Orange, New Jersey, SOMA Shares ran a used book drive where anyone in the community could drop off gently used books that were then offered to students at free meal pickup sites.

TIP

As much as possible, the books you provide shouldn't be the "I don't care if those books come back" books, but the good books. *Especially* the good books. When you provide students with coveted books that they can and want to read, you are saying, "Your reading life matters. And you matter." Kids need the real books, the full-color books, the representative books, the newly released books, the high-demand books. And they need them in their hands now.

Adapt Strategies for Students Who Are Reading E-Books

Why is this important?

When schools and public libraries closed for COVID-19 and we had a reading materials emergency on our hands, many schools turned to e-book databases to offer students access to something to read: Epic!, Libby, and Capstone Interactive to name a few. Although students can quickly find electronic titles on their devices, searching and filtering by interest, level, author, genre, and so on, and although some may even prefer reading digital texts, the interaction they have with e-books may not be as deep as it is with a print book they hold, turn pages, and cradle in their hands without some explicit teaching (Wolf 2018, 2020).

How do I do it?

In this new landscape in education, it's important to help students find the books and the format that best support their interests and comprehension—it's likely that digital texts will play some role. When students *do* read digital texts, you need to teach them strategies to support their comprehension. Spend some time looking at the most common strategies you teach and consider how they might (or might not) work differently when reading an e-book.

Bonus!

Check out Clare Landrigan's (2020) virtual book room where she has curated and organized freely available digital books into inviting virtual "baskets" for interest-driven browsing (http://bit.ly/3boJ3d7).

From *The Reading Strategies Book* (Serravallo 2015)	Modifications for E-Books
2.16: Choose Books with Your Identity in Mind	Rather than filter e-books based on level, consider other filters such as series, genre, author, topics, and themes.
5.14: Chapter-End Stop Signs	If your device is used for other things (email, Internet, FaceTime), you might be distracted by notifications. Make sure you're paying attention to your reading, specifically, the important events in your book. Jot down the important event(s) in each chapter off-screen before reading on to the next chapter.
8.7: Paraphrase Chunks, Then Put It Together	Rather than jot in the margins of the text, think about how you might record your paraphrasing. Can you "comment" into the document? Can you electronically bookmark the page and then jot your thoughts on a piece of paper? Would it be better to jot or sketch off-screen in a notebook?

Adapt Strategies for Students Who Are Listening to Audiobooks and/or Podcasts

Why is this important?

Audiobooks (some are even free with a library app such as Overdrive) and podcasts are widely available, and many students enjoy listening to them. When you welcome this alternative form of reading, you can confer with readers and teach toward their strengths and needs based on their listening comprehension. In fact, adding some audiobooks into a student's reading diet can help them engage in even deeper comprehension work.

TECH NUTS AND BOLTS

- Readers often highlight important text. With the **Audible** app, students can do this by selecting portions of the audiobook using the "clips" feature.
- You might ask older students to record their thinking as they listen: in a **Google Doc** they share with you, or in a notebook that they'll share with you during a conference (or take a photo of and upload).
- The *pause* and *play* buttons are great tools for conferring with students and having them practice and apply strategies. After I coached one reader to compare and contrast the characters in the story she was listening to, I invited her to play her audiobook from where she had just stopped listening. A minute or two later, she paused the book and tried the new strategy.

How do I do it?

To support students' comprehension in audiobooks, teach them strategies that support them in monitoring for meaning and visualizing while they listen/read in this medium.

From *The Reading Strategies Book* (Serravallo 2015)	**Modifications for Audiobooks and/or Podcasts**
2.6: Fixing the Fuzziness	Stop and jot or stop and sketch the who, the what, and the where, rather than marking a page with a sticky note.
5.9: Who's Speaking?	Sketch a picture of each character in your reader's notebook, or just write their name on a stick figure. As you listen to the dialogue being read aloud, point to the character who is speaking so you can better picture the speaker.
5.15: Where Am I?	Listen for setting clues in the narration or dialogue. Pause your audiobook to quickly picture the setting. Ask yourself, "What am I picturing it looks like there or then?" After you have a clear visual, keep listening.

Create Short Text Packets for Shared Reading Experiences

Why is this important?

There is power in a shared experience. As a class, when you read something together, you can use that text—the story, the characters, the vocabulary, the themes—to build a common understanding and support students with applying what they've learned to other texts. Similarly, when students read articles around a topic that connects to a content area, they can work together as they determine the main idea, key details, and the importance of text features. And in communities where kids do not have access to Wi-Fi or screens, text packets (of stories, articles, speeches, poems, etc.—*not* worksheets) can also provide supplemental material for independent reading.

How do I do it?

Think about some reading strategy or content area instruction that a text packet could serve, then assemble a collection of short stories, articles, and/or poems. You can send the packets to students as attachments to an email, upload them to your online platform, have them available for pickup, or print and mail them. You might plan to teach the strategy or content in a lesson, then have students follow up by practicing the strategy with the texts in the packet or digging into them with the content in mind. For example, in a first-grade classroom you might introduce a poem in a video or live class meeting, and then children could read and reread it (independently or with a partner over Zoom), practicing fluency as well as promoting community building.

What are some challenges?

A packet of texts is just not as ideal as baggies full of books, no question about it, but they do provide some shared content and they may be necessary and helpful in certain cases. If you intend for them to be used for students' independent reading, be sure to differentiate the collections for the students who will receive them and/or provide not only print copies but also audio versions. Keep in mind the interests of students and readability of the texts so that students will *want* to read them and *be able* to read them.

Rethink What It Means to Match Readers with "Just-Right" Texts

Why is this important?

When you're teaching remotely, you can't fine-tune students' text selection or their interactions with their texts the same way you do when they're in school. What you *can* do, however, is be flexible and try to celebrate how they are engaging with and comprehending what they've chosen to read.

How do I do it?

The how-to of this strategy is more attitude than action. Students' lives and reading lives have been altered, and it's more important than ever that you pay close attention to *how* they are engaging and making meaning as readers. Follow their lead, and then support them with what they need. For example, maybe you're noticing kids rereading books more than before you entered remote learning. This could be because they find comfort with familiar stories and topics, or it might be because their memory, stamina, and attention have changed during these difficult times. Familiar books, graphic novels, and shorter books are often helpful when students find it hard to slip into independent reading, so rather than discourage them, try to embrace whatever it takes for them to sustain their reading lives at home.

What else should I consider?

Remember that *independent practice* does not always need to mean *alone*. The social context of reading matters as it can support students' comprehension, always important, but especially during this time (Serravallo 2019). Book clubs may be just the thing students need to tackle a text that is too challenging for them to read or engage with by themselves.

During times of stress or change in environment (read: living through a pandemic), some may find it easier to stick with and comprehend shorter texts or a collection of essays. Others may gravitate toward books they've read many times before. Be flexible and help students find and access what will work best for them.

When students are reading remotely, they may pick up (or click on) books that you would have thought were too challenging or too easy for them in school, but this is a time to be extra flexible with your considerations and thinking. Students are drawn to books for all kinds of reasons.

Ask Students to Write Every Day

How much time do they need?

Similar to reading, I recommend you ask students to spend about twenty to thirty minutes each day writing, plus time to view any recorded lessons or participate in live lessons or conversations with peers.

How do I support them?

Most days, students' writing time will begin with them watching a minilesson you've recorded that supports your unit of study (see Chapters 3 and 6), and then they will move to writing independently. Other times, they may know where they left off with their project from the day before and get started on their own, possibly planning a virtual meet-up with you or peers later in the day, or knowing they can reach out during office hours if they get stuck. As they write, students work through the writing process at their own pace. Depending on the age of the student and the communication systems you set up, on some days they might read and respond to comments you've left in shared documents.

At least once a week, or slightly less frequently in middle school, students will have a video or phone conference (individual or small group) with you where they'll get feedback, get questions answered, and give you feedback on your teaching and how the unit is going for them (more on conferences and small groups in Chapter 6).

Partnerships and writing clubs can also be a helpful support as students work independently. Just as with book clubs, students may need some initial guidance from you, but as they become more independent with reaching out to friends for help and support, you may find (especially with older students or students with more involved caregivers) that they set meetings up on their own (more on partnerships and clubs in Chapter 6).

Writing time for this student is a balance of teacher and peer support and independent practice, with tech being used for connection, and writing happening off-screen.

Decide How Your Students Will Compose Their Writing

Why is this important?

Just because students are engaging in writing minilessons, small groups, and/or conferences on-screen does not mean that all of their composing also needs to be on-screen. Sometimes it will be helpful for students to compose in shared e-documents so that you can monitor their work and provide feedback and support. For younger writers, encouraging them to close their laptops and get out paper and writing implements can yield more, and better, writing.

How do I do it?

To make the decision about whether your students will compose on paper or compose on-screen, it's helpful to consider the advantages each one offers. On the next page are a few that come to mind. Can you think of others?

Composing on Paper vs. Composing On-Screen	
Some advantages of composing on paper	**Some advantages of composing on-screen**
Booklets and loose-leaf paper have a clear beginning, middle, and end, which supports students in organizing their writing.	The possibility of "talk to type" in certain extensions allows for some students to write more than they might with pen and paper.
Paper and pen do not require a device or Internet access, making it adaptable to the students' environment.	You and writing partners can offer feedback with ease in shared documents.
Paper and pen do not require word-processing skills, thus allowing some students to write more with a pen than they would with a keypad.	Students can coauthor writing by sharing texts with friends and writing partners, making writing more social.
With screens closed, composing is free of digital distractions.	Instant tools such as spell-check and grammar-check are available and may support composition.
Students can sketch on paper to plan out writing, and refer to sketches as they compose.	Fluent typists can get more words down per minute typing than handwriting.

TIP

You might invite your students to try both formats—composing on-screen and composing on paper. Ask them to reflect on their engagement and how much they were able to produce, as well as the quality of what they wrote, to determine which one is just right for them, keeping in mind that their preferences and productivity may change through a unit and across a year.

Give Students Access to Writing Materials and Tools

Why is this important?

If students are going to be composing their writing on paper, it's important they have the materials and tools to help them be successful. Consider what you have on hand for writers in the classroom, and therefore what they'll need at home:

- lots of blank paper, single pages and prestapled booklets (K–2)
- flaps of paper to add extra lines to a page (K–2)
- an alphabet chart (beginning writers)
- a stapler (for adding on new pages or making their own booklets)
- sticky note cover-up tape and colored pens for revision and editing work (and to make writing time more enticing and engaging)
- a writing folder to organize their work
- any copies of tools or resources (e.g., planning page, mini-charts, graphic organizers).

TIP

If getting these materials will be a challenge for your students, consider making individual "writing baggies" that you send home filled with the same kinds of supplies you use for writing in the classroom.

What do you mean by "blank paper"?

You might be wondering, "Shouldn't the paper have some sentence stems for students to complete or some writing prompts for them to respond to?" Blank paper and prestapled booklets offer students more choice and encourage a higher volume and better quality of writing. Students have the freedom to sketch, plan, and write the details that matter to them. A stack of blank booklets lets them know: your stories matter and must be told. Right here. Across these pages.

Young writers need to compose off-screen, with paper that supports the structure of the writing they are making. Encourage families to stay organized by housing their writing work in a folder.

Paper for kindergarten or early first grade offers a large space for drawing and labeling a picture.

Writing paper allows the student space on the page to sketch, and then later write on the lines. Teachers can offer various types with larger or smaller boxes and fewer or more lines, single sheets and/or prestapled booklets.

All writing paper choices shown are available for download at http://hein.pub/WSB.

Paper for procedural writing or for planning a sequenced narrative may include numbered steps.

Paper for informational writing can offer a variety of layouts so the writer can choose how to present the information.

Paper for poetry can have short lines to encourage line breaks.

A variety of paper templates are available in the online resources. Share them electronically with families to print out or mail them to students who don't have printers at home.

Strategy

Hold On (Tightly) to Writer's Notebooks

Why is this important?

Starting around grade 3, many teachers have students keep writer's notebooks where they make lists of possible writing topics, collect bits of interesting language, and try out all kinds of possibilities for their writing before they draft—outlines, leads, webs to develop characters, and so on. As Ralph Fletcher puts it, "A writer's notebook gives you a place to live like a writer, not just in school during writing time, but wherever you are, at any time of day" (1996, 4). Well, now that students are not actually in school, what better time for notebook writing to thrive!

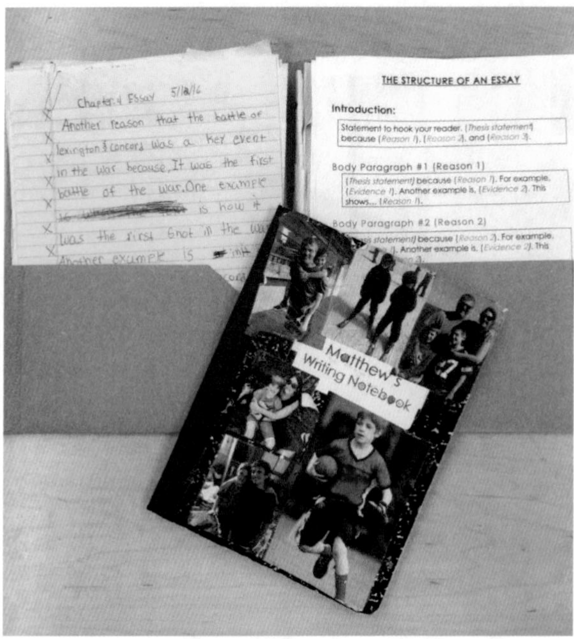

A notebook and folder are helpful materials for composing off-screen in addition to or instead of composing on-screen.

How do I do it?

Because they are meant to be used away from the desk, most writers keep physical, paper notebooks where they can write down their ideas and thoughts easily without Wi-Fi or access to a device. Physical notebooks allow writers to easily flip through many pages, remembering days and weeks of ideas to springboard new thinking, and they invite writers to compose in ways that may be more challenging or impossible on-screen: sketching, mapping, webbing. Notebooks are tactile and incredibly personal.

How do I do it online?

I recommend physical notebooks, but if getting them into your students' hands is just not possible, digital writer's notebooks are an alternative with some advantages, actually. With the click of a button in the digital notebook (use Google Docs or Slides), students can share their writing with teachers and peers and get immediate feedback or even collaborate on the same pieces. The technology makes it easy to upload photos and images for students to incorporate into their writing or inspire new stories.

What are some challenges?

Your students' preferences may not be universal. Check in with your writers and see when, how, and on what they do their best and most writing.

Set Up a System for Students to Share Some of Their Writing with You

Why is this important?

For you to assess student writing and offer feedback and coaching during conferences, you will need to be able to see some of the writing students are doing at home.

What do you mean, share "some" of their writing?

"Don't I need to see it all?" you might wonder. No, actually, you don't. It's fine for students to be doing more writing than you can keep up with during remote instruction. In fact, it's great if they are! What a perfect time for them to work on the novel they've always wanted to write, or make joke books, or compose song lyrics. Consider remote learning an opportunity for your students' independent writing lives to thrive.

How do I do it?

First you need to decide what writing you want to see from students and when you want to see it so you can communicate those expectations. Here are some questions to help you think about that:

- Do you want to see the writing before you plan to meet with the student? Or can you look at it together during your conference or small-group meeting?
- Do you need to see the whole piece of writing, or just a part of it?

- Will you specify what you want to see, or let students choose what they want to show you?
- Will you ask students to do any self-reflection before you talk about the writing they share with you?
- Will you need to keep the writing for any reason, or can it stay with the student after you've discussed/assessed it?
- If you do want to keep student writing, would an online portfolio (folder) for each student's work make sense?

TECH NUTS AND BOLTS

- **Seesaw:** Makes photographing and sharing work with the teacher easy for children, freeing up their grown-ups.
- **Flipgrid:** Start a grid and have children record short videos of themselves showing their work and/or reading it aloud.
- **Zoom** (or similar): During conferences and small groups, ask children to hold their writing up to the screen and read selected parts of it. You can take screenshots if you want to save it.
- **Google Docs** (or similar): For students composing on-screen, sharing documents is easy.
- **Email**: Students can attach most any kind of file, or they can embed their writing directly into the message.

Ask Students to Do Math Every Day

How much time do they need?

Just as with reading and writing, I recommend that students spend about twenty to thirty minutes a day on math, plus additional time to view recorded lessons, participate in live lessons, and/or to collaborate with peers.

TIP

Whenever possible, I recommend you use math manipulatives (either common objects found at home such as dried pasta, beans, or pennies as counters, or send manipulatives from the classroom home in "math baggies") for practice to help solidify an understanding with concrete objects, before moving to on-screen "manipulatives" (such as those available on Toy Theater) and eventually to abstract problem solving (O'Connell 2020).

Even though students may watch lessons online, encourage hands-on use of manipulatives off-screen to support concept development.

Bonus!

Sites such as Khan Academy or Greg Tang Math have free practice you can assign to students. Use these as a supplement to off-screen practice.

How do I support them?

I have done a lot of thinking and learning about math instruction as I've helped my own children during remote instruction. I think it's best to engage students in a math workshop, just as you do with literacy: start with a synchronous or asynchronous minilesson and follow it with independent practice. Schedule time during the week to work with students on math in conferences and small groups, and consider setting them up in partnerships to work together on problem solving.

How do I do it online?

Actually, as much as possible, I think practicing *off-screen* is best if it's manageable for your students. You might mail packets of math work home, send them digitally if students have printers, or direct students to work in a practice book (if they have them at home). If you must set students up for on-screen practice, encourage them to work out the problems on paper before they enter the answers on-screen.

Ask Students to Engage with Content Study Every Day

How much time do they need?

It depends. As you read in Chapter 3, sometimes you might integrate your students' reading and writing work with their content studies. At other times, when science and social studies are handled separately, I recommend students spend up to thirty minutes per day on content studies.

How do I support them?

You know by now that I recommend you get children off-screen as much as possible, and this is just as true with content study. Although you might have students watch a short video online (e.g., National Geographic or Brain Pop) or one of you teaching some content or doing an experiment, it can be helpful if the video prompts children to do something off-screen. Here are some science examples:

- Explore the ecosystem in your backyard or along your street.
- Find an insect to sketch.
- Do an experiment with melting ice cubes (in your refrigerator versus on the countertop) and record the data.
- Find different-shaped leaves and write in your science notebook comparing them.
- Find a ball in your house and play with different ramp inclines.
- Build a parachute with materials you have around the house and try launching an action figure out the window.

Suggestion!

Consider offering students texts or primary documents in science or social studies and then invite them to read, study, explore, record their questions and wonderings, create and share a presentation about what they learned, or engage in club-like discussions with peers.

What are some challenges?

Be mindful of the materials children will have readily available at home and the amount of support they'll need from caregivers to do the exploration as described—the simpler and more independent students can be, the better!

This young scientist tried growing seeds in two types of soil (with and without compost) and created a presentation to share, all off-screen. She used the device to connect with classmates, family, and the district's director of science, who were all invited to her presentation.

Plan for Students to Create and Move and Play Every Day

Why is this important?

Exercise and creative expression are crucial always and are especially essential in times of stress and crisis (Ahn and Fedewa 2011; Beauregard 2014; Jansen and LeBlanc 2010; Meyer DeMott et al. 2017).

How much time do they need?

You can suggest that students take short breaks for activity, play, or art intermittently throughout the day and/or help them to schedule blocks of time. You could also suggest one thirty-minute period for a "special" each day, in keeping with the special schedule in your classroom (e.g., Monday is art, Tuesday is PE, Wednesday is music, and so on).

How do I support them?

Hopefully your school has physical education, art, and music teachers who will share ideas, activities, and resources. Just remember to think about what off-screen materials students will need to be successful. As you work to send books, paper, and math manipulatives home, inquire about plans to send art materials, balls, jump ropes, recorders, Legos, and so on home as well.

If you wish to supplement what is being provided by the school with some additional physical education or performing or visual arts lessons and activities, do a quick search for children's illustrators and cartoonists

Bonus!

Go to http://bit.ly/3hyGabG for a helpful roundup of at-home resources for visual and performing arts, and more.

Go to http://bit.ly/2Quxbwl for a free "Handbook for Play in the Virtual Space" by Kristi Mraz (link to the handbook appears near end of blog post).

who have recorded lessons for kids at home (e.g., Grace Lin, Dav Pilkey, Mo Willems, Tom Watson, and more), check out major art museums that offer virtual tours and art lessons and invite children to be inspired to create their own pieces (e.g., Musée d'Orsay, National Gallery of Art, MASP, São Paulo), share links to dance or yoga classes accessible through YouTube (e.g., Cosmic Kids Yoga, Alvin Ailey Extension), and look for recordings of encore performances (e.g., Metropolitan Opera, Seattle Symphony, 92Y).

Lunch doodles with Mo Willems was a routine every afternoon in our house in the early days of quarantine. The regular invitation to create and laugh together was so therapeutic.

Chapter 6

Methods and Structures for Teaching Online

You know and rely on a variety of methods for teaching whole-class, small-group, and individual lessons when you're shoulder to shoulder with students in the classroom. This chapter shows you how to adapt those methods for online teaching and is filled with ideas to make conferences, minilessons, guided reading, strategy lessons, read-aloud, and more as high impact as possible when you're screen to screen. With the different instructional strategies, you'll see how to make your teaching and feedback clear and explicit, how to monitor your students' progress, and how to sustain meaningful connections with your learners.

A really important point before you dive into this chapter: these are *options*. You will have to decide which strategies feel most comfortable for you and are most likely to engage your students; planning for multiple pathways is crucial (www.cast.org; www.understood.org). What you choose to reach and teach some children may not be what you choose for others.

Also, you don't need to implement this all tomorrow. Really. Browse through and find something that feels accessible to you right away, or something you feel is close to what you already do but you want to tweak, or something you think would have an immediate positive impact, or one idea that feels interesting—and give it a try. Just as you do with your students, you should set small, manageable goals for yourself. Check back to Chapters 4 and 5 to see how these pieces fit into a possible daily schedule.

Throughout this chapter you'll see that I suggest tech tools (e.g., Zoom, Flipgrid, Padlet) as well as tech functions (e.g., breakout rooms, chat boxes). I haven't tried to cover all the options with these suggestions; instead, I stick close to the few tools I've gotten comfortable using. I recommend you find your small set of tools and use them over and over again, too. The emphasis in this chapter, as I hope it is with you and your students, is on the art and craft of your teaching; the technology is just a tool.

TECH TIP

When choosing the tech tools you'll rely on most, learn the type(s) of device(s) your students will use and any limitations the tech may have on those device(s). For example, Zoom works best when a user downloads a software package which isn't possible on Chromebooks. With the browser version possible on the Chromebook, students can't use functions such as grid view, emojis, or click hyperlinks shared in the chat box.

Develop Community Agreements and Norms for Participating Online

What are community agreements and norms?

Agreements developed by the community for the community to detail how everyone will feel safe, cared for, and able to work their best in the online environment. They are most effective when they are co-created with learners (Casimir 2020; Hoffman, Bracket, and Levy 2020; National School Climate Center 2007).

How do I do it?

Anticipate potential challenges of working together in an online space. Talk with your students in advance about the norms you need to establish together. Consider discussing:

- how to enter and leave online meeting spaces
- how to ask a question or advocate for yourself if you need help
- how to invite someone to participate
- how to get attention in a meeting without disrupting someone else's flow of thought
- that it's OK for students to turn off their camera, mute themselves, and/or step away if they need privacy or become overwhelmed

- accommodations for students who wish to engage without turning their cameras on (such as through the chat box)
- expectations for breakout rooms, especially if you are in a "room" without the teacher
- how to find a spot against a wall or change the background so students have privacy and don't reveal anything about their home environment that they don't want to reveal
- side conversations and private chat messages, and the kinds of comments that can harm the learning environment.

What are some challenges?

All norms must be discussed, taught, and practiced before you can expect students to manage them on their own. Once you get started, issues may come up that you didn't anticipate and you'll need to revise the norms you've established.

TIPS

Be sure to invite students to give you feedback if something about the community agreement isn't working for them.

As a general rule, you might ask students to agree not to say anything online that you wouldn't say to someone's face, in the company of family members and teachers.

Set Yourself and Your Students Up for Videoconferencing

Why is this important?

Videoconferencing, whether meeting with the whole class, small groups, or individuals, gives your students a chance to connect with friends and classmates in real time and you a chance to see and hear your students. For your synchronous meetings to work effectively, you'll need to explicitly teach students how to get set up for videoconferences (and follow this advice yourself!).

How do I do it?

Students need to learn how they can best see, hear, and interact with you and their classmates in videoconferences.

Video

Lighting: Sit with your face to the window, not with light at your back. If you're recording in a dark room or closet, or at night, you might want to experiment with desk or standing lamps you have or invest in a ring light.

Camera angle and framing: Make sure that your camera is several inches above your head and pointed down (I accomplish this by setting my laptop on yoga blocks). Make sure you sit close enough to the camera that it's easy to see you and your facial expressions. Some may find it helpful to show your torso as well to allow children to see hand gestures.

Background: Seeing many people on-screen at once can be distracting for everyone, and some might feel it's an invasion of privacy. Set up with your back to the wall, or other neutral background, or learn to change your background.

Sound

Location: Set up in a quiet room with the door closed if at all possible.

Headset: Use headphones or a headset with a microphone when a quiet room isn't available.

Mute: Keep yourself on mute when you are not speaking. As the presenter, use the "mute all" feature to avoid accidental interruptions.

Viewing and Pinning

View: Familiarize yourself with the grid view versus speaker view in your preferred videoconferencing software. Direct students to choose one over the other depending on the type of session (e.g., conversations like book clubs are best in grid view, minilessons are best in speaker view).

Pin: Learn how to "pin" the speaker and teach students to pin your video when you're delivering a lesson.

Self View: Teach children how to turn off their "self view"—staring at oneself can be distracting or even off-putting.

Convert Your Live Minilessons to Recorded Microlessons

What is a mini/microlesson?

In the classroom, minilessons—periods of direct instruction—are typically about ten minutes long, but with online instruction it's best to keep them *micro*—two to three minutes ideally (and no longer than five). When you keep your teaching succinct, you make it more likely students will stay engaged with the content and you also free up time for other types of instruction and feedback.

What are some challenges?

In the classroom, minilessons typically start with a demonstration that lasts a few minutes, followed by a chance for children to practice while you listen in and provide feedback and support. With online recorded lessons, you'll need to tighten up and shorten the demonstration, and also figure out how students will practice without you being right there with them.

How do I do it?

Use the minilesson structure, abbreviate it for online teaching, and convert existing minilessons into microlessons.

Attention!

Research shows that attention falls off after watching a video for six minutes, and that the optimum length for student engagement is around the three-minute mark (Brame 2015).

Synchronous / Live Minilesson (10 minutes)	Asynchronous / Recorded Microlesson (2–3 minutes)
Connection (1–2 minutes)	**Connection (30 seconds)**
• Make a connection between prior work and today's work. • Tell a story that serves as an analogy. • State the strategy.	• Quickly connect to the unit goal or yesterday's lesson. • State the strategy.
Teach (2–3 minutes)	**Teach (1–2 minutes)**
• Set up the demonstration. • Model in your own book or writing, use a mentor text. Voiceover. Think aloud. • Give an example or explanation.	• Explain how to try the strategy. • Offer a quick example or think-aloud.
Active Engagement (2–3 minutes)	**Active Engagement (30 seconds)**
• Set students up to practice. • Listen in, coach, give feedback as they practice. • Share what you heard.	• Skip it. *Or* • Invite children to rewatch the video. *Or* • Prompt kids to pause the video and try something.
Link (30 seconds)	**Link (30 seconds)**
• Restate the strategy. • Remind students of other strategies they know.	• Restate the strategy. • Remind students of other strategies they know.

Microlesson Tips

Be animated—use facial expressions and vary tones in your voice.

• • •

Use quick ***homemade visuals*** to anchor learners to your key points.

• • •

You may be tempted to produce perfect video clips, but clear and correct is good enough. ***Avoid rerecording*** a half dozen times for a minor verbal stumble or quick interruption from your toddler—save your time so you have more to give to synchronous teaching, feedback, office hours, and guided practice.

• • •

Resist the urge to make elaborate slide decks or graphics—seeing your face, and maybe a hand-drawn quick visual anchor, will do.

• • •

Teach children how to do, versus just ***what*** to do. Demonstrate or explain step-by-step strategies that children can go off and practice independently.

An Idea!

After watching some of your lessons, students may want to start making their own to share with friends. You can start a "student teacher" library of tip clips to direct students to learn from peers.

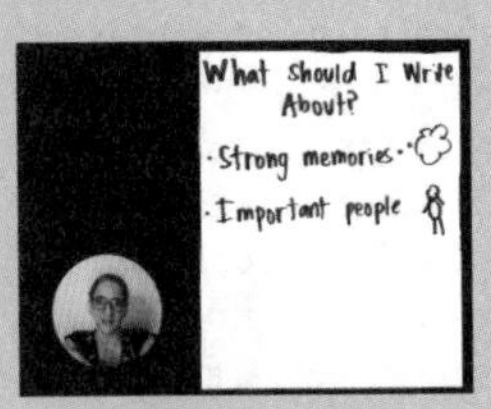

VIDEO 6.1
Barb's four-minute lesson was made with Loom in under ten minutes. Did you hear the thunder clap at the end? She didn't rerecord!

TECH NUTS AND BOLTS

- **Zoom, Google Meet, or Microsoft Teams:** Open a room just for yourself and record your lesson. Post the recording to the class Learning Management System.
- **Screencastify:** Record right from your browser. Annotate on top of what you are sharing, enable your webcam, publish directly to your Learning Management System. Saves automatically in your Google Drive.
- **Loom:** Another Chrome extension, similar to Screencastify, but with a free app that you can download on your phone or tablet. One way to use Loom is to prerecord your teaching demonstrations on your phone, then open the app and record your teaching on top of them. Essentially, your demonstration becomes the background until you hit play on it.
- **Make a homemade document camera:** Connect a second device (phone, tablet) to your computer to broadcast onto your desktop using an app like iDocCam, or screencast one device on another (available with Apple). You can then record your video and what's in view using your "document camera."

Make Your Microlessons More Engaging

What do you mean by "more engaging"?

Have you ever watched a popular YouTube channel? A famous TikToker? If you're like me, you wonder, "Why am I watching this?" and yet, you can't stop. It's not so much the content as it is the *way in which it's filmed*. There's a craft to it. YouTubers can sell ad spots the longer they keep you watching, and they've figured out *how* to keep you watching.

What are some challenges?

My biggest challenge is I know *zip* about video editing, and the viral YouTube videos all look highly edited. But this is also an important time to remember that a premade video starring anyone *but* you will likely not have the same effect. You may be enticed to buy lessons that have been prerecorded by someone other than you, or to use not-you recorded lessons that you find online. But your children want to see *you*, their actual teacher, now more than ever. Plus, in the time it takes to find and preview videos, you can just make your own for free!

How do I do it?

All my worries about my lack of video-editing skills melted away the day I found the app Clips (an Apple product). You can record your two- to five-minute lessons and change the background, add captioning and animations, play with filters and special effects, add background music, set it to create automatic captions, and more. I figured it out the first

Tips for Engaging Microlessons

Record everything right into the app, or pull photos or videos from your camera roll.

Toggle between kids seeing you and kids seeing something else (text, book cover, object that serves as an analogy for whatever you are talking about, sticky note with the strategy written on it) and try to say no more than a sentence or two for each image.

Aim for two to three minutes; max out at five.

Play with different filters, stickers, music, and effects.

time I tried it—it couldn't be more intuitive. Then my daughter saw me, grabbed my phone, and made one herself (again, no instruction, she just intuited how to use it). You'll have fun, be proud of the finished product, and your students will be amazed!

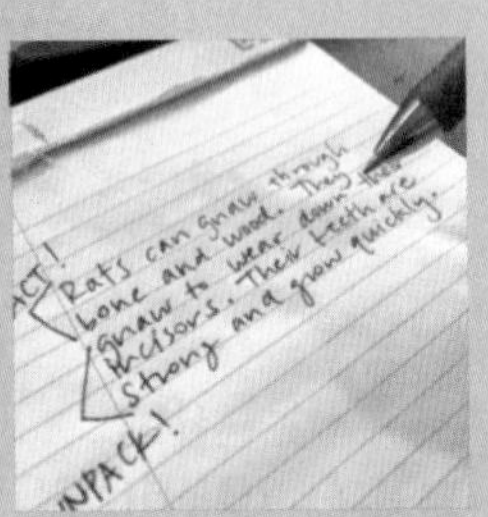

VIDEOS 6.2 AND 6.3
My first two attempts at creating Clips lessons—a writing one on unpacking facts, and a reading one on the mood of settings.

TECH NUTS AND BOLTS

- **Clips:** A highly intuitive, user-friendly, on-your-device video-creating app. If you don't have an Apple product, do a quick search for an app similar to Clips for your device.

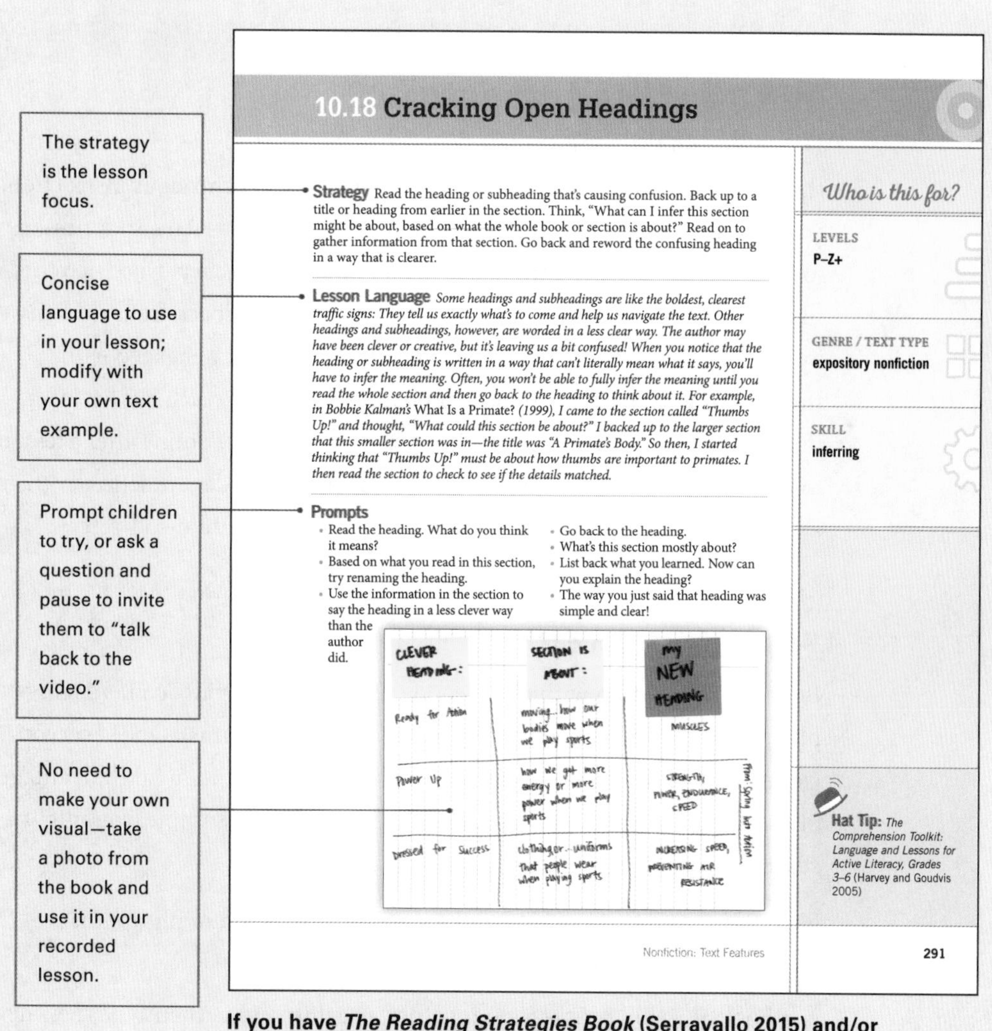

10.18 Cracking Open Headings

Strategy Read the heading or subheading that's causing confusion. Back up to a title or heading from earlier in the section. Think, "What can I infer this section might be about, based on what the whole book or section is about?" Read on to gather information from that section. Go back and reword the confusing heading in a way that is clearer.

Lesson Language *Some headings and subheadings are like the boldest, clearest traffic signs: They tell us exactly what's to come and help us navigate the text. Other headings and subheadings, however, are worded in a less clear way. The author may have been clever or creative, but it's leaving us a bit confused! When you notice that the heading or subheading is written in a way that can't literally mean what it says, you'll have to infer the meaning. Often, you won't be able to fully infer the meaning until you read the whole section and then go back to the heading to think about it. For example, in Bobbie Kalman's* What Is a Primate? *(1999), I came to the section called "Thumbs Up!" and thought, "What could this section be about?" I backed up to the larger section that this smaller section was in—the title was "A Primate's Body." So then, I started thinking that "Thumbs Up!" must be about how thumbs are important to primates. I then read the section to check to see if the details matched.*

Prompts

- Read the heading. What do you think it means?
- Based on what you read in this section, try renaming the heading.
- Use the information in the section to say the heading in a less clever way than the author did.
- Go back to the heading.
- What's this section mostly about?
- List back what you learned. Now can you explain the heading?
- The way you just said that heading was simple and clear!

CLEVER HEADING:	SECTION IS ABOUT:	my NEW HEADING
Ready for Action	moving... how our bodies move when we play sports	MUSCLES
Power Up	how we get more energy or more power when we play sports	STRENGTH, POWER, ENDURANCE, SPEED
Dressed for Success	clothing or... uniforms that people wear when playing sports	INCREASING SPEED, PREVENTING AIR RESISTANCE

From: Spring into Action

Who is this for?

LEVELS
P–Z+

GENRE / TEXT TYPE
expository nonfiction

SKILL
inferring

Hat Tip: *The Comprehension Toolkit: Language and Lessons for Active Literacy, Grades 3–6* (Harvey and Goudvis 2005)

Nonfiction: Text Features 291

If you have *The Reading Strategies Book* (Serravallo 2015) and/or *The Writing Strategies Book* (Serravallo 2017), you have all you need to make your own microlesson from any page.

Monitor and Guide Students' Independent Practice

Why is this important?

Depending on the number of students you work with, the level of support they need, and your students' ability to connect for synchronous instruction, you may at times choose to meet children live online to teach a short lesson followed by some guided and independent practice. Teachers who tried this in the spring said that they felt like they got helpful feedback from students by kidwatching (Goodman and Owocki 2002) while they engaged with their learning, and doing so made it possible for kids to reach out for in-the-moment support and guidance. Plus, when students stay online after a lesson to read or write, you've carved out the time for independent practice *for* them and can get them going with practice that they then continue off-screen.

How do I do it?

Begin by connecting with children via your preferred videoconferencing platform (e.g., Zoom, Google Hangouts, Microsoft Teams). Once everyone is gathered, do a live one- to two-minute demonstration, then take advantage of the opportunity to lead some guided practice. For example, you might ask students to do things such as:

- Hold their notebooks up to the screen with a word or phrase that responds to a prompt.
- Look at a skill progression together, use it to revise, then type their new responses into the chat box.
- Move into breakout rooms to turn-and-talk with partners while you "visit" a couple of partnerships to listen in to their conversation.

Important!

If you're going to have students join you online live for the lesson, try to make it as interactive as possible so you can give feedback and also assess and get feedback from your students.

After the seven- to ten-minute lesson with guided practice, set a timer for about twenty minutes and ask students to start their independent practice (e.g., take out their books to read, take out their notebooks to write). You might even display a timer on-screen. Then you can work with them in one of several configurations (depending on the options your videoconferencing tech makes possible):

- Your whole group can read/write/practice together, with their mics muted, while you observe them as they work. Then you might:
    - Invite students to ask questions that come up by typing into the chat box.
    - Prompt all your students to stop and jot something in the chat box (to avoid students using other students' answers in their own, you can direct them to send the note to you only).
    - Prepare a list of students you wish to confer with and, one at a time, ask them to unmute and turn their volume up. Some teachers use a bright-colored sign held up to the camera to get a student's attention.
- You can move students into small breakout rooms with a few other students to read/write/practice. Then you might:
    - Invite students to ask a friend in their room if they need help.
    - Move from room to room to confer with individual students. The other students in the room can listen in, benefiting from the conference they overhear.
- You can use a breakout room just for individual conferences, have students "meet" you there, then return to the whole class to continue practicing.

Tips for Synchronous Workshops

Let students know before the session starts who you'll confer with that day. You might post a list of names in Google Classroom or make an announcement before students start working independently.

Aim for each conference to last about five minutes; if you set everyone up to practice for about twenty minutes you'll be able to meet with four students during that time.

To monitor multiple rooms at once as you confer, you can join the same meeting(s) from two different devices to have access to them both.

Anytime you teach a synchronous lesson, you will have students who aren't able to join for a variety of reasons. ***Be sure to record your lesson*** and upload the video into your online learning platform (e.g., Google Classroom, Canvas, Schoology) so all students have access.

If you don't have breakout room capability, you can create different meeting codes for whole-class work and conferring (for example, "3DMeets" for the whole class and "3DConfer" for conferences). Have the students you are conferring with that day sign out of the whole-class meeting after your lesson and into the conferring meeting.

When the independent practice time is up, you can bring everyone back together by asking them to mark their ending page, and then perhaps type an important thought they had or something they tried in the chat box. You might share out a few key responses, reiterate what you taught in the minilesson, and/or share something that came up during your conferences.

What are some challenges?

Not every student will experience this method of teaching the same way. Some might share that the experience was mildly distracting; others might say that it felt like they were in a much-needed classroom community and that it helped them to engage and have the teacher available for questions. Be sure to ask students how the sessions are going, and depending on the feedback you get, you might decide to shift away from this type of monitored independent work time, or to continue it for a select group of students.

TECH NUTS AND BOLTS

- **Breakout rooms:** Check to see if your videoconferencing software has this function and be sure to enable them in your settings in advance if it does.
- **Chat box:** A great way to engage children and get instant feedback without the inevitable delays that come from turning mics on and off.
- **Screen share:** Consider what visuals can anchor your work together—slides, skill progressions, a shared text, and so on. Share from your desktop or connect another device that functions as a document camera.
- **Annotation tools:** Get comfortable with annotation tools that help you circle, write, draw, and point to spots on-screen where you want children to focus.
- **Emojis/thumbs up/clapping:** Get instant feedback and encourage participant engagement.
- **Polls:** Within Zoom you can set up quick in-the-moment check-ins with polls ahead of time, or use a polling tool like Mentimeter, which will allow children to see live results of the poll on-screen.

Read Aloud (Live!) to Build Community

Why is this important?

Prepandemic, read-aloud was a versatile tool that helped you

- Build community in your classroom.
- Support students' growing comprehension and conversation skills.
- Assess students' thinking and speaking work in a low-pressure, high-interest way.
- Show children how to use strategies from your curriculum.

In the face of so many challenges that come with virtual teaching, read-aloud is one of the structures that doesn't really need to change that much to still do all this important work. You can hold a live read-aloud lesson with your whole class or with small groups of students.

How do I do it?

For read-aloud, gather the whole class, half the class, or a group together on the videoconferencing platform of your choice and make sure they are all on mute. Children in grades 2 and above should come to the session ready to write.

Just as you would for live, in-person teaching, plan ahead where you will stop and ask children to participate in some way (e.g., act out, turn and talk, stop and jot). The trick is, for an online read-aloud, you will need

Consider This:

Children learn a lot about reading fluency from hearing a skilled and proficient reader read, so sometimes you might just do a story time-style read-aloud without stopping to prompt children to talk, jot, or act parts out.

to invite children to participate in ways that are possible with the tech tools of your videoconferencing software. You might prompt children to:

- Give a thumbs up or raise a hand on-screen, just like they do in the classroom, to signal "me too!" or "I'm ready!" or to ask to be called on.
- Share their thinking with an adult or sibling who is in the room with them (or even a stuffed animal or pet!).
- Get up, move around, and quickly act something out.
- Use an emoji to show their reaction.
- Move into breakout rooms for conversation with a partner or small group.
- Type a quick response in a chat box.
- Write something on a whiteboard and hold it up to the camera.
- Type into a Google Form (and then you can share the responses by screen sharing).

Read-Aloud Tips

Ask open-ended questions that require children to think (e.g., "How is the character changing?" rather than "Where did the character go in the last chapter?").

Keep your stopping and prompting lean and quick, and then get back into the book.

Vary the length of the books you are reading. Consider reading a picture book on one day (or across days).

When reading a chapter book across weeks, remember the ***power of suspense***. Try to stop each read-aloud in a place that makes children excited to pick up where you left off.

Make sure your ***book choices*** consider your students' identities and offer them opportunities to see themselves (mirrors) and better understand others (windows) (Bishop 1990).

If you are utilizing a curriculum that is recommending specific titles that you do not have at home, ***find an appropriate substitute***, starting with titles you love (and have access to). To widen your access to books, sign up for an online book database.

Record Read-Aloud to Engage, Support Comprehension, and Collect Data

Why is this important?

When you record a read-aloud and share it with your students, you can leverage many of the same benefits you get from reading aloud either in person or synchronously online. This option can be a lifeline if your students face challenges to joining you for synchronous instruction.

What are some challenges?

Without your students in front of you as you're reading, you might wonder if they engaged with the text, how much of the video they watched, or if they comprehended as they listened. Sometimes you'll want to capture their thinking or response to the video.

How do I do it?

While recording yourself reading aloud seems pretty straightforward, there are a few options to consider:

- You might record yourself reading a text for children to simply listen to and enjoy. Remember that this kind of read-aloud is valuable, too—you're modeling fluent reading and a love of books.
- To support comprehension, pause during the recording to think aloud and model strategies; prompt children to think, or even turn and talk (to a sibling, pet, or stuffed animal). You can also invite children to have conversations with friends about the book on their own, in book clubs, or in partnerships (see pages 145–147).

Bonus!

Invite a surprise guest reader to join your class. You can often find videos of authors reading their books on their YouTube or Instagram pages, or well-produced readings by a well-loved personality on Storyline Online.

- To utilize read-aloud as an assessment tool in grades 2 and above, create opportunities for children to stop and respond in some way—jot or sketch on a sticky note, share out/act out with a video response, and/or post their responses (see Tech Nuts and Bolts, page 135). Once you collect students' responses, sort like responses together to drive your small-group instruction, look across responses to think about class-wide trends that can inform future read-aloud and mentor text study sessions, or collaborate with colleagues to think about trends across the grade and how to revise curriculum.

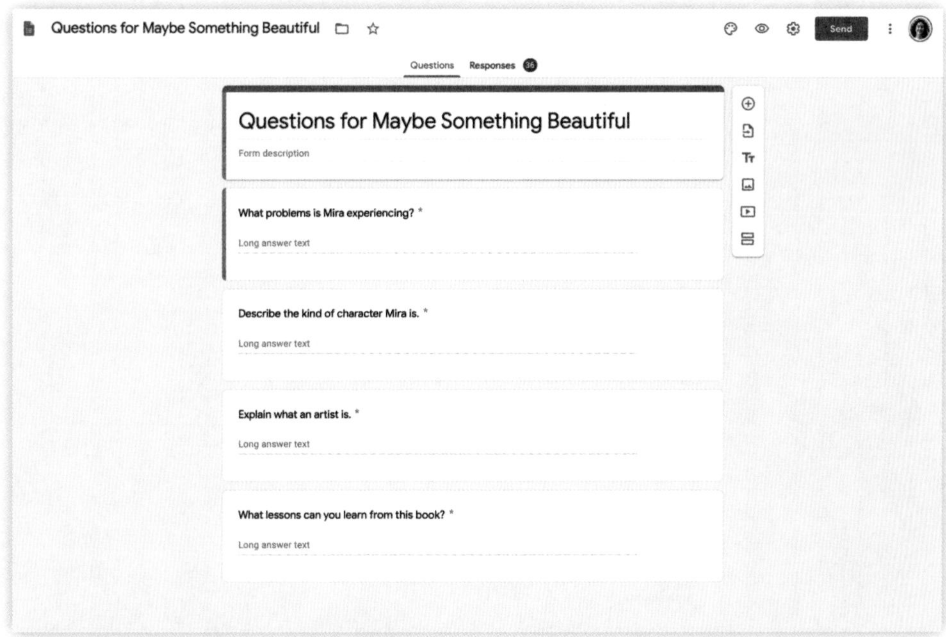

This simple four-question Google Form captured a class' thinking during a read-aloud.

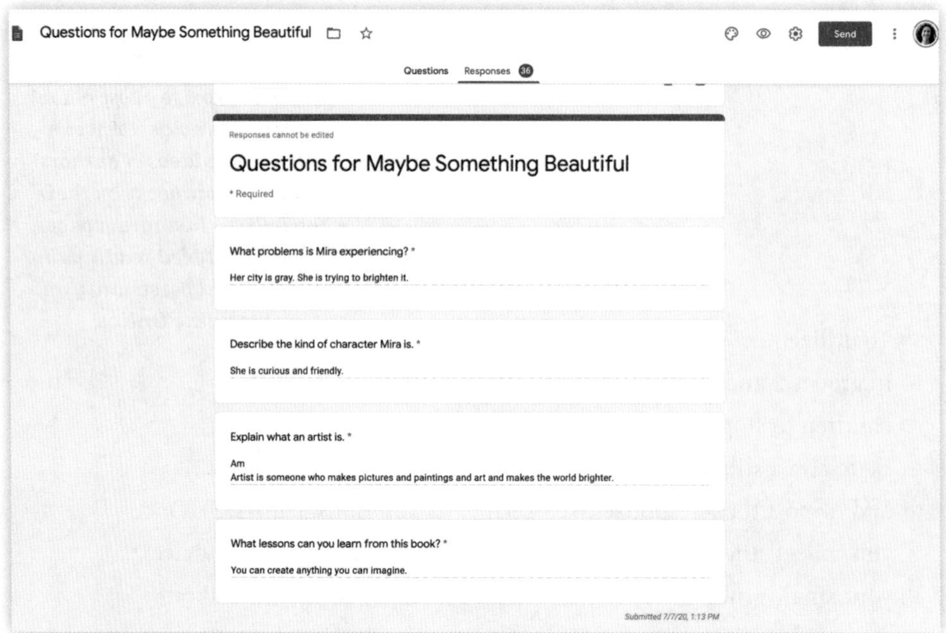

Once students respond, view by individual (to help with goal setting, planning for conferences, or groups).

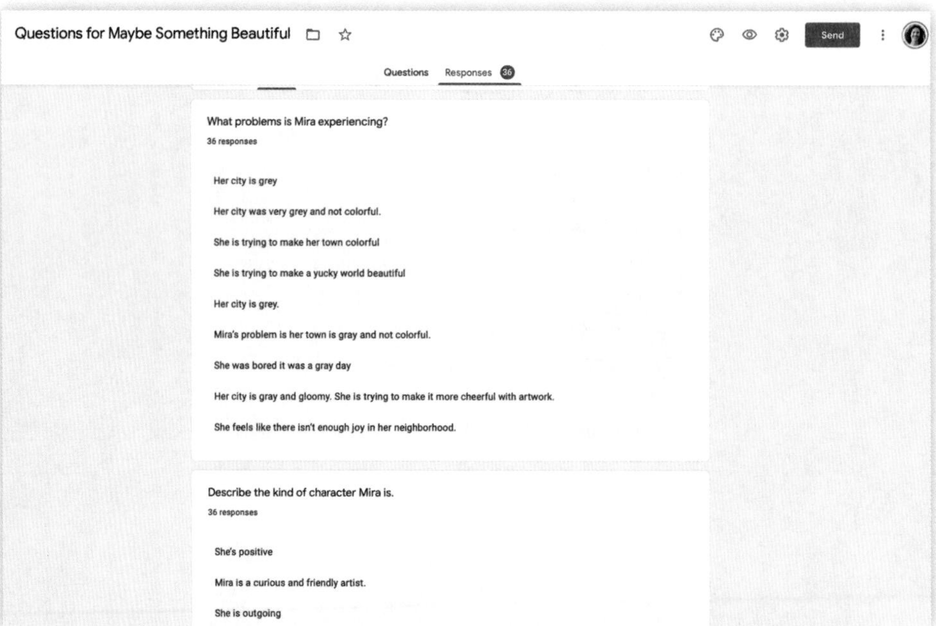

Look across the class' responses (to notice trends for whole-class lesson planning).

TECH NUTS AND BOLTS

- **Zoom:** Record yourself reading aloud and hold the book up to the screen, or use Screencastify and a document camera to display both the book and you.
- **Google Forms:** Set up a form with open-ended questions and prompt children to stop and jot in the form at various points during the read-aloud video or at the video's end.
- **Edpuzzle:** Insert stopping places into a video to prompt students to respond.
- **Flipgrid:** Record and upload a video that children respond to with their own video.
- **Padlet:** Collect digital sticky notes under headings.
- **Seesaw:** Children can take a photo of a sticky note, record a video, or use a computer trackpad/device screen to jot or draw. Your kindergarteners to second graders can find success with this device-friendly option for turning in work.

Study a Mentor Text for Writing Craft

Why is this important?

Just as it does in your classroom, studying a mentor text online with your whole class or a small group of children encourages them to notice and name writing craft that they might try out in their own writing. With mentor texts you can emphasize and reiterate key goals from your unit and support students with a real-world example to inspire their own work.

VIDEO 6.4
Watch this lesson with a group of eighth graders studying a mentor text with me in a small group. They have the text in a separate window on-screen and I use my phone as a document camera to display shared notes.

How do I do it?

Select a passage that provides examples of the writing work (craft and genre) students are doing in your writing unit. Make sure you've thought ahead about the "moves" the writer has made that you hope children will see.

With children gathered online and muted, make sure they can see the passage clearly on the shared screen, or send a link to the text that they can open in a separate browser window or print out ahead of time. Introduce the text and read it aloud once so all can access it. During the second read, prompt students to notice and name the writer's craft, and take notes on what they say. After the lesson, make your notes available on your online platform and invite students to try out any craft "moves" that make sense for their own writing.

TECH NUTS AND BOLTS

- **Screen share** or **document camera:** Make sure the focus is on the text and that all children can see it clearly. Screen share or use a second device set up as document camera to display the page or send a link to the text that students can open in their own browser window or print in advance.
- **Annotation tools:** Helpful for marking up the text on the shared screen as you talk about it.
- **Breakout rooms**: If you're meeting with a larger group, you may want to send them to breakout rooms to discuss, and then come back to share what they noticed with the whole group. Note that you can't share texts in breakout rooms, so you'll need to send students a link with the text in advance, and/or encourage them to print out a copy to mark up off-screen.

Mentor Text Study Tips

Choose a short passage or portion of a longer passage students will be excited to study.

Choose a passage that has ***writing moves*** that you think children can try out on their own.

Open up the conversation by demonstrating how to read like a writer, if this is new for your students.

Ask students to name what *they* see, versus them naming back what *you* see. Questions like "What else is the author doing?" and "What do you notice?" are good starting points.

Send a link to the digital text for children to print out and mark up off-screen if possible.

Confer with Students Live

Why is this important?

Conferring helps you do the important work of seeing the rich and beautiful variety of individuals and to honor and cherish where each student is with their learning (Paley 2000). Connecting one-on-one allows you to value each child's language and literacy practices and their own literacy development and to treat each child as a competent learner (Ladson-Billings 2009; Souto-Manning and Martell 2016). You become a researcher as you learn about your students, and they learn from you, blurring the lines between teacher and student (Morrell 2012; Freire 1998). Now, more than ever, the magic is in the connections you are able to make with your students and the feedback you are able to give them—and that they are able to give you.

How do I do it?

You can use conferences to set goals, assess, coach and guide practice, and more, and they can be used in any subject area (Serravallo 2019). Each type of conference has a unique structure and purpose, with consistent student and teacher roles, but regardless of which conference type you choose, they have a few things in common. During conferences:

- **Students** are expected to self-reflect, show what they've learned, ask for support, and practice strategies.
- **Teachers** offer new strategies or support for ones still being practiced, give feedback, and guide learners.

One of the most common and versatile conference types is the Research-Compliment-Teach conference. Its predictable structure helps you stay focused and be impactful. Here's the structure with just one minor adaptation for conferring online:

VIDEO 6.5
Watch an example of me conferring with a kindergartner.

VIDEO 6.6
Watch an example of me conferring with a rising sixth grader about uncovering themes in her chapter book.

1. ***Connect.*** Spend a minute or two connecting with the student about something unrelated to literacy. Ask them what they've been up to with a sibling, how the banana bread they were going to bake turned out, if they've been on any bike rides, how they're finding space in their home to work. This is not something you'd typically do in a conference in the classroom because you likely have many other points throughout the day when you are connecting with children like this. In the online classroom, when individual or group meetings are less frequent, it pays to nurture relationships before launching into academics.
2. ***Research.*** Ask questions connected to the student's goal. For example:
   a. Ask them to hold work up to the camera, or look together at a shared document (such as a Google Doc).
   b. Share your screen with a text displayed and ask them to read aloud.
3. ***Compliment.*** Notice something the student does well and is helping them accomplish their goal. Name it clearly (e.g., "I see you are . . .").

4. ***Teach.*** Keeping in mind a skill progression, offer the student a strategy to build off their strength.

5. ***Coach.*** Give the student a chance to practice. Provide prompts, feedback, and support. Balance your teacher talk with their practice. Provide wait time.

6. ***Link.*** Repeat what you worked on together. Name their work as a series of steps and give the child an opportunity to name the strategy in their own words. Add a visual for the strategy to any digital notebook or communication or note-taking app you are using. For example, in a Google Doc you could add a comment next to where the student practiced to remind them of their strategy, or take a photo of a sticky note you jotted and add it into their Seesaw folder.

TIMING TIP

In the classroom, conferences are typically five minutes long and you aim to see each student multiple times a week; with online schooling you might aim for a fifteen- to thirty-minute block of time to confer with each student once a week. This gives you time to check in and see how students are doing, longer guided practice time, and/ or time to confer in multiple subject areas. A long block of time also simplifies scheduling for you and your students; just be sure to give movement breaks.

What are some challenges?

Scheduling live conferences can be a challenge, especially for students who work with multiple teachers, or for those families with multiple children (and multiple schedules!) in the home. It helps to have a predictable schedule (e.g., Isabel meets with you every Wednesday at 10 a.m.) or to allow students to sign up for a time that works for them, and to remind families of the schedule (and the link to join the conference) in your weekly correspondence, as well as to post the schedule in an easily accessible place in your Learning Management System. See more on scheduling conferring time in Chapter 4.

TECH NUTS AND BOLTS

- **Videoconferencing:** You can set up a "room" with one link to share with all students, and give them a scheduled time to join, enabling a "waiting room" so that any new student who joins isn't interrupting or listening to the conversation between you and another student. Alternatively, set up individual links for each child.
- **Phone:** When access to Wi-Fi or devices is inconsistent, offer a phone conference as an option.

Confer with Students When Your Schedules Don't Align

What do you mean, "when schedules don't align"?

Conferences are designed to be live conversations between a teacher and student. However, if meeting with certain students in real time is challenging, you may need to get creative and try an "almost-conference" using some tech tools to assist you.

What are some challenges?

The biggest challenge here is, of course, not being able to give feedback to students in real time as they practice.

How do I do it?

Here's how an asynchronous almost-conference might go, along with some timing suggestions meant to help you keep it manageable:

1. ***Research*** (one minute). Study the work the student has sent you related to their goal. For example:
    - a sample of writing
    - a recording of them reading aloud to demonstrate how they are using their fluency or decoding strategies
    - a recording of a retelling of their book
    - photos of the sticky notes or writing about reading they've done.

2. ***Compliment and Teach*** (two minutes). Send a video to the student, using the same app or means of communication the child has used (see Tech Nuts and Bolts). You could also provide some quick written feedback in an email or document comment, with a link to a quick recorded lesson that explains or demonstrates a strategy that would be relevant and responsive to the student's next steps.

3. ***Link*** (thirty seconds). Invite the student to reach out with questions and give them a deadline to send back something that shows what they have worked on based on the conference. Encourage them to rewatch your video or reread comments for reminders.

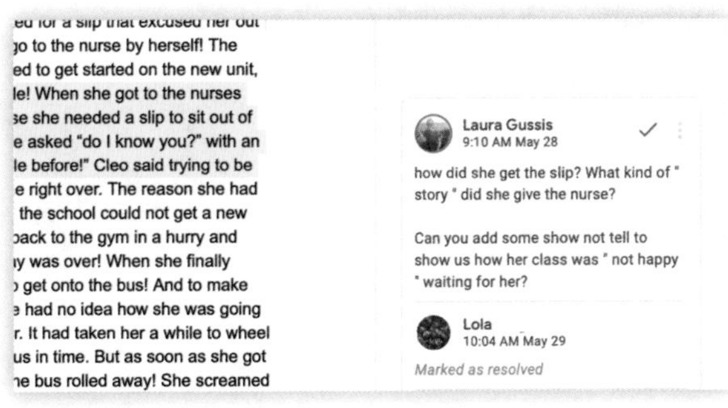

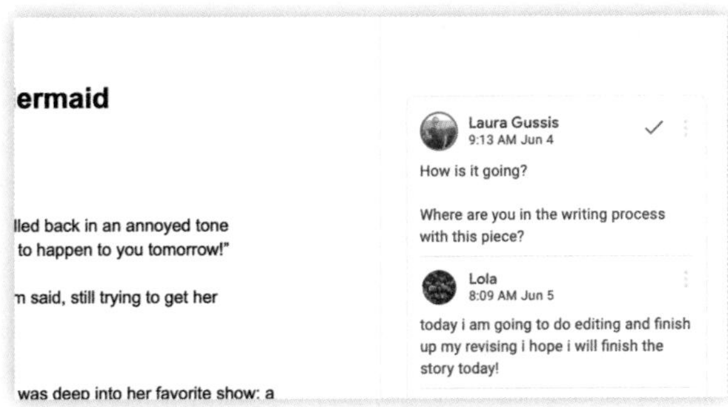

When meeting live is challenging, "conferring" through notes in a document can help. Be sure to be explicit and offer clear step-by-step strategies for any new learning, and consider providing a link to a video with a short demonstration.

TECH NUTS AND BOLTS

- **Google Docs:** Students draft and share their document, and you can "confer" through comments. Any videos you want to show can be shared through a link.
- **Email:** Students (or their grown-ups) email you their work or a video of them talking about their writing, or reading, or reading aloud. You respond through a written email or with a video.
- **Flipgrid:** You can create a grid for each student and correspond through videos that you share with each other, back and forth.
- **Seesaw:** Younger students can easily navigate this app to send written work or videos.

Set Up and Support Reading and Writing Partnerships and Clubs

Why is this important?

Reading and writing independently each day at home can get lonely. Reading and writing partnerships and clubs can offer so much: motivation and accountability, help getting "unstuck," support, a critical reader of your writing when you need it most, someone to recommend your next book, and more. Even the most engaged and independent among us benefit from connecting with friends.

During writing-focused partnerships and clubs, students can support each other with any step of the writing process. They can:	During reading-focused partnerships and clubs, students can:
• Come up with new ideas. • Field ideas ("I was thinking of writing about . . . what do you think?"). • Rehearse aloud before drafting. • Give critical feedback to inform revisions or edits. • Celebrate small successes and/or a published piece. • Make plans and promises for their writing lives.	• Share a text on-screen and read together (taking turns with pages, acting out parts like reader's theater, choral reading). • Come ready to talk about favorite parts, reactions to characters, big ideas about themes or issues that show up in the text. • Recommend and book talk other books. • Discuss the read-aloud text (if text access is something you're still working on). • Make plans and promises for their reading lives.

Suggestion!

You can use any of the strategies in Chapter 10 of The Writing Strategies Book *(Serravallo 2017) or Chapter 12 of* The Reading Strategies Book *(2015) to support and elevate the work of any K–8 reading or writing partnership or club.*

How do I do it?

Flexibility is key. In your classroom you likely set children up in partnerships and clubs based on their goals, by the level of text they are reading, or by the sophistication of their writing. But in the online classroom, you may need to do more to support students' engagement—pair them based on friendships or common interests so they are encouraged to meet even when they aren't being led by you. Or—just ask your students who they want to partner or be grouped with!

VIDEO 6.7
A first-grade book club watched a video of *Marvelous Cornelius* (Bildner 2015) read aloud and then got together to discuss.

To support partnerships and groups, you'll need to meet with them from time to time and adapt your conferring for the online space:

1. ***Connect.*** Greet the students who have entered the online meeting space and connect with them personally for a moment or two.
2. ***Research.*** Invite the students to begin their work—discussing a book, sharing the screen and reading together, sharing a piece of writing and giving feedback, and so on. If the group needs help getting started, offer a prompt such as, "Why don't we start with Monique's piece? Monique, will you share your screen and read the part you'd like feedback on?" Once students are interacting, take a moment to just observe and take notes on how they are working together; view their practice through the lenses of conversation/collaboration as well as reading or writing skills.

3. ***Decide.*** Choose something to point out that the group is doing that will be helpful to continue to do, and something that you can teach them.
4. ***Compliment.*** Offer a clear, explicit compliment.
5. ***Teach.*** Offer the students a strategy that you want them to practice immediately.
6. ***Coach.*** Prompt and give feedback as they practice the strategy you taught them. Try to stay focused on just that strategy.
7. ***Link.*** Remind students what they practiced. Perhaps have them jot down a note in their notebooks to remember the strategy, and/or add notes to whatever online note-taking system you're using. Encourage the group to meet again, without you, and let them know when you'll see them again.

TECH NUTS AND BOLTS

- Partnerships and clubs can meet using your district's approved videoconferencing software. Although screen sharing capability may be helpful at times, groups don't need breakout rooms or the chat box or other features. Remind them about using a grid view and disabling their self-view to keep their focus on their peers.

TIMING TIP

Conferring with groups and partnerships in the classroom usually takes about five minutes. You may find they take more time online (as much as ten minutes). To make scheduling easier and to save time with transitions, you might decide to meet with the same group about reading *and* writing in a longer twenty- to thirty-minute block of time. See more on scheduling in Chapter 4.

Engage Reading Partnerships and Clubs with "Written Conversations"

What is a "written conversation"?

"Written conversation" (Daniels and Daniels 2013) is pretty much just what it sounds like—a conversation in writing. Many of us engage in written conversations every day through text messaging. In the classroom, you might put a large piece of chart paper in the middle of a table and invite reading partners or club members to write ideas and questions down, using one color each. The "conversation" continues as children circle and add onto ideas with lines and arrows. The end result looks like a spider web of insight. Since written conversation unfolds more slowly than spoken conversation, students have a chance to go deeper as they ponder before providing a response.

What are some challenges?

For some students, pen and paper is more efficient than typing. Digital "written conversations" may be extra challenging for those students who are in the beginning stages of becoming proficient with a keyboard.

How do I do it?

Written conversations are easily adapted for the online classroom. To get one started, invite a reading partnership or club to join in a shared online document or interactive slide deck where a "topic under discussion" is written on its own page or slide. Students choose their own color or font to differentiate their ideas, and then they add their thoughts and ideas in text boxes connected to the starter idea.

Consider This:

You might find children need some guided practice the first time they try this new structure, or you might find that they are like my ten-year-old daughter who, when denied her own cell phone, decided to start "texting" (a written conversation!) in a Google Doc with her best friends from school.

What do you think about Claudia being jealous of Janine more than Janine being jealous of Claudia?

I think Claudia and Janine fight because they are jealous of each other.

What makes you say that?

My sister and I fight when we feel jealous of each other.

Or maybe they are fighting because they are so different.

That's true. But don't opposites attract? All the members of the BSC are so different but they are BFFs.

Fourth graders each used a different color when adding onto an interactive shared slide, connecting one thought to the next.

TIP

You can encourage the use of memes, emojis, clip art, and more in written conversations, or you can ask students to keep it just to text. And just as you would encourage respectful language in the classroom, remind children of your co-created norms and agreements for online learning (see pages 116-117), and to be mindful of the impact of their words in this online space.

TECH NUTS AND BOLTS

- **Google Slides, Docs, or Jamboard:** Students type, draw, and annotate directly onto a shared page. They can keep their conversations in a shared Google folder.
- **Padlet:** Students can collaborate on a board by typing their responses directly to one another, or they can jot their ideas down, take a photo of their work and upload it. Kids can also take a photo of a page from a book they are referencing and upload it into the conversation.

Engage Writing Partnerships and Clubs with Written Feedback

Why is this important?

In the classroom, students engage in the give-and-take of response throughout the writing process, both informally as they're working and when they meet in established partnerships and clubs. But when they are writing at home, students don't have that same kind of immediate access to their classmates' feedback. In the case of a writing "emergency," they have to problem solve on their own as they await their peers' response. Teaching students to give each other written feedback is one way to help them feel supported as writers even when they're far apart.

How do I do it?

The simplest, most straightforward way for students to comment on each others' work is to comment in a shared document like Google Docs or through an email exchange. Another option is for students to record short videos (using Flipgrid, for instance) and talk through their response to share with a classmate. Consider teaching students to follow a structure for their feedback, such as:

1. Praise: Share at least one thing they feel works well.
2. Wonder: Ask one question about something that's unclear.
3. Polish: Offer one piece of feedback for something to improve.

You might adapt strategies (or create new ones) that students can use to give and receive feedback in the online environment. For example, the following strategies from *The Writing Strategies Book* (Serravallo 2017) can be adapted for asynchronous written partner or club feedback.

Strategy	How you might use it to support asynchronous feedback
10.5: Make Promises (You Can Keep)	This strategy is about students sharing their writing goals with a partner, and having that partner check in with them to hold them accountable and (hopefully) celebrate when they achieve their goals. This can happen through email or in-document comments just as it can happen in in-person conversation.
10.6: Partner Inquisition (to Get Your Thinking Going)	Rather than interrupting their partner with prompts as they read their piece aloud, teach students to add challenge questions into comments in a shared document ("What else happened?"; "Can you say more?"; etc.).
10.9: Help Wanted/ Help Offered	Instead of a corkboard in school with "job" listings, you might create an online list to matchmake experts with those who want to learn something. Maybe in Padlet, in an interactive slide deck, or in a shared Google Doc.

TECH NUTS AND BOLTS

- **Flipgrid:** Students can record videos and share ideas and responses back and forth.
- **Marco Polo:** Children can record videos and share back and forth on a smartphone or tablet.
- **Google Docs:** Engage in written conversation using the comments feature within a shared document.
- **Email:** Teach students how to attach drafts or embed them in the body of an email.

Engage Partnerships and Clubs with Asynchronous Video "Conversation"

What do you mean by "asynchronous video conversation"?

It's a mouthful, I know. Keeping kids connected to one another is crucial during remote learning, but it can be challenging to help them establish and maintain these social connections if they are all on different schedules. With asynchronous video conversations, your students can engage with texts and each other, responding to video with video, on their own time.

VIDEO 6.8
This book club of fifth graders sends video messages about what book they want to read next.

Why is this important?

In their book, *180 Days* (2018), Penny Kittle and Kelly Gallagher share about a prepandemic, cross-country book club they did inviting teenagers in Conway, New Hampshire (Penny's students), and Anaheim, California (Kelly's students), to connect through Flipgrid. On opposite sides of the country, their students read the same book and had back-and-forth conversations by recording short videos.

I heard Penny and Kelly talk about this at a National Council of Teachers of English conference a few years ago, and they said the experience was highly engaging for so many reasons—their students got to connect with students with very different backgrounds and experiences in a different state, they grappled with big issues presented in their book club books, and they especially enjoyed taking selfie videos!

How do I do it?

Once students are comfortable recording and sharing videos (see Tech Nuts and Bolts), then you'll just need to support them with some strategies for conversing in this online format. The following strategies from *The Reading Strategies Book* (Serravallo 2015) can be adapted for asynchronous conversation about books.

Strategy	How you might use it to support asynchronous conversations
12.9: Conversation Playing Board	Each child selects an idea they've jotted during their independent reading and types it at the top of a Padlet page. Others respond by recording their own videos or using the voice-recording option. Alternatively, you could use a Google Slide deck. Each child "starts" a conversation on a slide with an idea from their book, and other students record quick videos and paste them into the slide.
12.10: Sentence Starter Sticks	Nobody will be pulling a stick from a jar online . . . but you could offer some sentence starter phrases ("I agree . . ."; "I'd like to add on . . ."; "On the other hand . . .") for students to use when they are recording video responses to others.
12.21: Bring On the Debate	If you have children discussing issues online where there may be disagreement, you'll want to teach them about respectful language and ways of responding to each other—even if those responses are in recorded video.

Bonus!

When book clubs meet in person, a student's ability to process the conversation quickly and respond in real time might make them feel reluctant to speak, uncertain, or shy. With asynchronous clubs, they have time to think and then record their ideas and responses when they feel ready.

TECH NUTS AND BOLTS

- **Flipgrid:** Partners and club members can record short video responses to one another. You can visit to monitor progress, assess, and leave private text feedback.
- **Padlet:** Students can create a discussion board and share resources, type notes, and/or record and post short video responses to one another.

TIP

You don't need to make the same decision about whether to do book clubs live or asynchronously for every student in your class, nor do your decisions need to be fixed. Personalities, schedules, and more might influence which children will thrive within each, and when.

Meet with a Small Group of Students with the Same Goal (Strategy Lessons)

▶ VIDEO 6.9
Watch this small-group strategy lesson with a group of fifth graders who are working to come up with topics for summer writing projects.

What is a strategy lesson?

Strategy lessons are versatile: they are a great choice in any grade level and can be used to teach strategies to support just about any skill or goal in any subject area, just like one-on-one conferences. In a strategy lesson, children are grouped because they would all benefit from instruction and guided practice around the same strategy.

How do I do it?

When setting up small-group strategy lessons, you can either form the groups based on your assessments and set a schedule ("Marcus, Shana, and Veronica—meet me online at 9:30 a.m. Tuesday and here's the link"), or you could invite students to sign up for the topic(s) that most interest them and/or are aligned to their goals. (See more on scheduling in Chapter 4.)

During the lesson, a predictable structure helps you keep your lesson focused and impactful:

1. ***Connect.*** Spend a minute or two connecting with your students on a personal level. Let them do most of the talking and practice empathic listening.

2. ***Teach.*** Remind students of their goal, what the topic is that they signed up for, and/or why you've convened them. Be clear about the strategy you'll offer (breaking it down into a step-by-step how-to), and make sure it's not book or writing piece specific.

Advice!

Keep your coaching efficient so you can get to each student in the short session. Think more oscillating sprinkler versus gardening hose.

3. ***Coach.*** Give students a chance to practice while you offer prompts, feedback, and support. I have found the best way to do this is to put each student in their own breakout room. Then, I can move from room to room and have conversations without distracting the other students. Another option is to have children turn down their sound (but not off) as they're working, then turn their volume up to participate in coaching. This method can be more distracting than breakout groups, but it does have benefits: you can easily keep an eye on the other children, and sometimes overhearing a peer's feedback is helpful.

4. ***Link.*** After the coaching period, pull the students back together, repeat the strategy clearly, and set the expectation for what students will do on their own after the meeting. Add a visual for the strategy to a note-taking app, or ask older students to jot down the strategy in their own words and have them show you their notes.

TECH NUTS AND BOLTS

- **Breakout rooms:** Set them up ahead of time and remind students how the session will go. When you are with them in their "room," you will coach them; when they are working independently, they are working by themselves.
- **Note-taking:** Take notes in between coaching individual students or when the small group has ended and you are getting ready for your next one.

TIMING TIPS

Small-group strategy lessons typically take seven to ten minutes in the classroom, but online you may want to allot more like fifteen minutes. Students might straggle into the meeting room a bit late, there may be some tech glitches that need to be ironed out, there can be delays in audio or video feeds that cause you to have to ask students to repeat themselves, and so on.

When you're just starting out with synchronous differentiated teaching in the online environment, it may be easier to schedule individual meetings (conferences) rather than groups. Once you better know and understand students' needs, grouping them becomes easier.

Move Your Guided Reading Online

What is it?

Guided reading is a small-group structure where you are scaffolding students' reading development across a series of increasingly complex texts. Guided reading, like all reading instruction, should be assessment driven. Children are grouped together based on the level of text they will be reading. You choose the text carefully and plan for what you'll teach based on what each child is ready to take on.

How do I do it?

One of the biggest stumbling blocks to virtual guided reading lessons is a logistics problem. How do you give students copies of the one title you want them to read with you during the session? To help solve this problem, I recommend you use online e-books, like Epic! or Reading A–Z.

Here's the basic structure and some logistics you can use for the lesson:

1. ***Connect.*** Greet the children, and then spend a minute or two connecting with them on a personal level.
2. ***Introduce.*** Share your screen as you introduce the text and give support for what is new and what might be tricky—e.g., elements such as genre, graphophonic work, vocabulary, and sentence length. Help children activate their background knowledge and make predictions about the text. Before you direct them to read independently, you may also introduce a strategy or give a clear focus or purpose for reading.

3. *Read and coach.* When kids are ready to start reading on their own, share a link to the text in the chat box. Teach them how to open up the text in one window and keep the video call in another. Place each child in a breakout room, and then move from room to room and have them read to you while you give them assessment-based feedback tied to their individual goal.
4. *Discuss/wrap up.* Close the breakout rooms and pull students back together into the main meeting room. You might have them retell, discuss what they learned from the book, or teach a quick strategy.

What are some challenges?

Some children may need help from an adult with the logistics of all this, especially the first time. If you know a child doesn't have at-home tech support, you might choose to work with them one-on-one rather than in a guided reading group until they get the hang of it.

Similarly, if you use a videoconference platform that doesn't have breakout room capability, I think it would be best *not* to do guided reading as a group. If children all have to stay in the same meeting room, taking turns reading aloud while you coach them will feel and function like an outdated practice that's not supported by research: round robin reading. You can still meet with children one-on-one with a text you've selected. You could also record book introductions to send to several children, and then hop on a one-on-one meeting to do the reading and coaching part only to save time.

Guided Reading Tips

In your classroom, guided reading lessons typically take around twenty minutes—a long time for young children to be in a videoconference. For guided reading online, aim for more like fifteen minutes, which probably means you *read less text* together. You can also break up longer texts into a series of lessons that stretch across sessions.

When you are coaching an individual student, make sure the other students know to keep reading on their own. Make sure students know to restart the book if they happen to finish it during your session.

Plan your *book introduction* ahead of time so you can deliver it clearly and succinctly.

Limit the size of your online guided reading groups to three to four students. The more children you include, the less time you will have with each of them.

Use your assessments to inform your grouping, book selection, and text introduction.

Encourage students to reread the text you used for guided reading on their own.

Apply the Tech Tools and Strategies You've Learned to Lead Any Type of Group Online

Why is this important?

In your classroom, you probably do all kinds of other small-group work that I haven't described here. My hope is that after reading this chapter, you feel empowered with teaching moves and tech tools so you can bring your classroom approach to the online space.

How do I do it?

Let's think about some of the general advice around synchronous and asynchronous teaching from this chapter:

- Adapt how much time a lesson takes online versus in person (in general, recorded lessons need to be shorter and you should allow for more time when teaching live!)
- Consider what tech tools to use for connecting live (choose your videoconferencing software).
- Think about what tech tools to use for connecting asynchronously (just learn one to start—maybe Flipgrid, Padlet, or a Google Doc).
- Choose the bells and whistles within the tool you might use (for example, for live teaching, consider if breakout rooms, chat boxes, screen sharing, etc. fit with the type of lesson you want to do).

An Example: Shared Writing	In a shared writing lesson, you work live with students, elicit ideas from them, and "hold the pen" to scribe what they say. How can you use what you know from this chapter to apply it to this lesson type? You will need: • a way to connect visually (videoconferencing) • a way for students to see the text you're co-composing (use a Word document with screen sharing or write on paper and use a doc camera or other connected device) • use of the chat box for children to share their suggestions (if they are somewhat fluent at keyboarding) or ask them to unmute to talk. (If the latter, probably best to keep the group smaller, rather than trying to meet with the whole class.)
An Example: Phonics or Word Study Lessons	Think about how you teach phonics and word study. Do you need to display a set of words or letters for all students to see? Do children need to be able to see your mouth clearly? Do you need any shared tools such as an alphabet chart? How will you keep children actively engaged in a live lesson? Chances are, you'll need: • a prepared slide deck with words or letters • charts with the phonics principles you're teaching on-screen (or on paper with a plan to share using a doc camera) • online manipulatives (See Toy Theater for example, or set up a Jamboard) and/or manipulatives sent to children's homes ahead of time • the ability to write on-screen and have other children see.

Works Cited

Ahmed, Sara. 2018. *Being the Change: Lessons and Strategies to Teach Social Comprehension*. Portsmouth, NH: Heinemann.

Ahn, S., and A. L. Fedewa. 2011. "A Meta-Analysis of the Relationship Between Children's Physical Activity and Mental Health." *Journal of Pediatric Psychology* 36 (4): 385–97.

Amer, Aly A. 1997. "The Effect of the Teacher's Reading Aloud on the Reading Comprehension of EFL Students." ELT Journal 51 (1): 43–47. https://academic.oup.com/eltj/article-abstract/51/1/43/417035?redirectedFrom=fulltext.

Beauregard, C. 2014. "Effects of Classroom-Based Creative Expression Programmes on Children's Well-Being." *The Arts in Psychotherapy* 41 (3): 269–77.

Bildner, Phil. 2015. *Marvelous Cornelius*. San Francisco, CA: Chronicle Books.

Bishop, Rudine Sims. 1990. "Mirrors, Windows, and Sliding Glass Doors." *Perspectives: Choosing and Using Books for the Classroom* 6 (3): ix–xi.

Blum, Susan D. 2020. "Why We're Exhausted by Zoom." *Inside Higher Ed*. April 22. www.insidehighered.com/advice/2020/04/22/professor-explores-why-zoom-classes-deplete-her-energy-opinion.

Brame, Cynthia J. 2015. "Effective Educational Videos." Vanderbilt University, Center for Teaching. https://cft.vanderbilt.edu/wp-content/uploads/sites/59/Effective_Educational_Videos.pdf.

Brooks, Robert. 2003. *Self-Worth, Resilience, and Hope: The Search for Islands of Competence*. Metairie, LA: The Center for Development and Learning.

Calkins, Lucy, and colleagues. various. Units of Study series. Portsmouth, NH: Heinemann.

Casimir, Arlène E. 2020. "Lessons from Crisis: Trauma-Responsive Teaching Tools for the Work Ahead." ASCD. June 8. https://inservice.ascd.org/lessons-from-crisis-trauma-responsive-teaching-tools-for-the-work-ahead/.

CAST. n.d. "About Universal Design for Learning." www.cast.org/our-work/about-udl.html#.XybYfC85Q4c.

Center for Collaborative Classroom. 2020. "Beginning-of-Year Guidance for the 2020–2021 School Year: Responding to the Impact of School Closures." www.collaborativeclassroom.org/wp-content/uploads/2020/06/BOY_CSC-Guidance_2020-2021_PL4966.pdf.

Cipriano, Christina, and Marc Brackett. 2020. "Teachers Are Anxious and Overwhelmed. They Need SEL Now More Than Ever." EdSurge. April 7. www.edsurge.com/news/2020-04-07-teachers-are-anxious-and-overwhelmed-they-need-sel-now-more-than-ever.

Cohen, Jonathan, Libby McCabe, Nicholas M. Michelli, Terry Pickeral. 2009. "School Climate: Research, Policy, Teacher Education and Practice." *Teachers College Record* 111 (1): 180–213. www.researchgate.net/publication/235420504_School_Climate_Research_Policy_Teacher_Education_and_Practice.

Daniels, Harvey A., and Elaine Daniels. 2013. *The Best-Kept Teaching Secret: How Written Conversations Engage Kids, Activate Learning, Grow Fluent Writers . . . K–12*. Thousand Oaks, CA: Corwin.

Diamond, Adele, and Kathleen Lee. 2011. "Interventions Shown to Aid Executive Function Development in Children 4 to 12 Years Old." *Science* 333 (6045): 959–64. www.ncbi.nlm.nih.gov/pmc/articles/PMC3159917/.

Ebarvia, Tricia. 2020. "Connect the Dots." *Tricia Ebarvia* (blog). May 31. https://triciaebarvia.org/2020/05/31/connect-the-dots/.

Equity in Action Committee. 2020. "Equity Guide for Pandemic Schooling: An Action Guide for Families, Educators, & Communities." July 30. https://drive.google.com/file/d/1UcUOcbsqZlKFv8fI6ehU4RuKiUcjz_-O/view.

España, Carla, and Luz Yadira Herrera. 2020. *En Comunidad: Lessons for Centering the Voices and Experiences of Bilingual Latinx Students.* Portsmouth, NH: Heinemann.

Fisher, Douglas, Nancy Frey, and John Hattie. 2016. *Visible Learning for Literacy, Grades K–12: Implementing the Practices That Work Best to Accelerate Student Learning.* Thousand Oaks, CA: Corwin.

Flaherty, Colleen. 2020. "Zoom Boom." *Inside Higher Ed.* April 29. www.insidehighered.com/news/2020/04/29/synchronous-instruction-hot-right-now-it-sustainable.

Fletcher, Ralph. 1996. *A Writer's Notebook.* Portsmouth, NH: Heinemann.

Freire, Paulo. 1998. *Teachers as Cultural Workers: Letters to Those Who Dare to Teach.* Boulder, CO: Westview Press.

Godoy, Maria, and Daniel Wood. 2020. "What Do Coronavirus Racial Disparities Look Like State by State?" NPR. May 30. www.npr.org/sections/health-shots/2020/05/30/865413079/what-do-coronavirus-racial-disparities-look-like-state-by-state.

Goodman, Yetta, and Gretchen Owocki. 2002. *Kidwatching: Documenting Children's Literacy Development.* Portsmouth, NH: Heinemann.

Gordon, Berit. 2020. *The Joyful Teacher: Strategies for Becoming the Teacher Every Student Deserves.* Portsmouth, NH: Heinemann.

Gray, Peter. 2020. "Survey Reveals Children Coped Well with School Closure." *Psychology Today.* August 3. www.psychologytoday.com/us/blog/freedom-learn/202008/survey-reveals-children-coped-well-school-closure?fbclid=IwAR2a9IqzI4AsMyT-qo8H_mcSs1rVhV1ZZYRIdopXFXQqdW1SdrDKvHhOARg.

Greenberg, Brian. 2020. "What We've Learned from Distance Learning, and What It Means for the Future." *Education Next.* June 2. www.educationnext.org/what-weve-learned-from-distance-learning-what-it-means-for-future-improving-online-education/.

Ham, Jacob. 2017. "Understanding Trauma: Learning Brain vs. Survival Brain." July 25. https://drjacobham.com/videos.

Hammond, Zaretta L. 2014. *Culturally Responsive Teaching and The Brain: Promoting Authentic Engagement and Rigor Among Culturally and Linguistically Diverse Students.* Thousand Oaks, CA: Corwin.

Harvard University. n.d. "Teach Remotely—Best Practices for Online Pedagogy." https://teachremotely.harvard.edu/best-practices.

Hattie, John, and Shirley Clarke. 2018. *Visible Learning Feedback*. New York: Routledge.

Heard, Georgia. 2016. *Heart Maps: Helping Students Create and Craft Authentic Writing*. Portsmouth, NH: Heinemann.

Herrmann, Erick. 2014. "The Importance of Guided Practice in the Classroom." February 12. https://exclusive.multibriefs.com/content/the-importance-of-guided-practice-in-the-classroom/education.

Hill, Grace. 2020. "The Pandemic Is a Crisis for Students with Special Needs." *The Atlantic*. April 18. www.theatlantic.com/education/archive/2020/04/special-education-goes-remote-covid-19-pandemic/610231/.

Hoffman, Jessica, Marc Brackett, and Scott Levy. 2020. "How to Foster a Positive School Climate in a Virtual World." EdSurge. May 21. www.edsurge.com/news/2020-05-21-how-to-foster-a-positive-school-climate-in-a-virtual-world?fbclid=IwAR21J7vXtUSzfYHUmgmKuwl1O24R-oxX40XsQUOjLSRvNNBQ9YnxrCeeOEk.

Hollinghead, Aleksandra, and Davin Carr-Chellman. 2019. "Engaging Learners in Online Environments Utilizing Universal Design for Learning Principles". *eLearn*. February. https://elearnmag.acm.org/archive.cfm?aid=3310383.

Homework Gap Coalition Letter to Congress. July 22, 2020. https://educationvotes.nea.org/wp-content/uploads/2020/07/Homework-Gap-Coalition-letter-to-Congress-7.22.20.pdf.

Howard, Jaleel R., Tanya Milner-McCall, and Tyrone C. Howard. 2020. *No More Teaching Without Positive Relationships*. Portsmouth, NH: Heinemann.

Institute of Museum and Library Services. 2020. "Research Shows Virus Undetectable on Five Highly Circulated Library Materials After Three Days." June 22. https://www.imls.gov/news/research-shows-virus-undetectable-five-highly-circulated-library-materials-after-three-days.

International Society for Technology in Education (ISTE). n.d. "Online Teaching Microcourses + Bundles." www.iste.org/isteu/microcourses.

Jansen, I., and A. G. LeBlanc. 2010. "Systematic Review of the Health Benefits of Physical Activity and Fitness in School-Aged Children and Youth." *International Journal of Behavioral Nutrition and Physical Activity* 7 (1): 40.

Johansen, Dana, and Sonja Cherry-Paul. 2016. *Flip Your Writing Workshop: A Blended Learning Approach*. Portsmouth, NH: Heinemann.

Jones, Stephanie P. 2020. "Ending Curriculum Violence." *Teaching Tolerance Magazine* (Spring): 64. www.tolerance.org/magazine/spring-2020/ending-curriculum-violence.

Kamenetz, Anya. 2020. "The Biggest Distance-Learning Experiment in History: Week One." NPR. *All Things Considered*. March 26, 4:17 p.m.

Kendi, Ibram X. 2016. "Why Standardized Tests Have Standardized Postracial Ideology." American Association of University Professors. November–December. www.aaup.org/article/why-standardized-tests-have-standardized-postracial-ideology-.Xyc6Mi85Q4c.

Kittle, Penny, and Kelly Gallagher. 2018. *180 Days: Two Teachers and the Quest to Engage and Empower Adolescents*. Portsmouth, NH: Heinemann.

Krause, Kaitlin. 2020. "Emotionally Connected Learning Is Possible Online. Start with Relationships." EdSurge. July 14. www.edsurge.com/news/2020-07-14-emotionally-connected-learning-is-possible-online-start-with-relationships.

Ladson-Billings, Gloria. 2009. *The Dreamkeepers: Successful Teachers of African-American Children*. San Francisco: Jossey-Bass.

Laho, Nora S. 2019. "Enhancing School–Home Communication Through Learning Management System Adoption: Parent and Teacher Perceptions and Practices." *School Community Journal* 29 (1). www.adi.org/journal/2019ss/LahoSS2019.pdf.

Landrigan, Clare. 2020. "What Could Be Better Than a Virtual Classroom Library? A Virtual Bookroom!" www.clarelandrigan.com/blog/what-could-be-better-than-a-virtual-classroom-library-a-virtual-bookroom-booklove-bettertogether.

Lieberman, Mark. 2020. "Virtual Education Dilemma: Scheduled Classroom Instruction vs. Anytime Learning" *Education Week*. March 30. https://blogs.edweek.org/edweek/DigitalEducation/2020/03/synchronous_or_asynchronous_e-.html.

Love, Bettina. 2019. *We Want to Do More Than Survive: Abolitionist Teaching and the Pursuit of Educational Freedom*. Boston, MA: Beacon Press.

Meyer DeMott, M. A., M. Jakobsen, T. Wentzel-Larson, and T. Heir. 2017. "A Controlled Early Group Intervention Study for Unaccompanied Minors: Can Expressive Arts Alleviate Symptoms of Trauma and Enhance Life Satisfaction?" *Scandinavian Journal of Psychology* 58 (6): 510–18.

Milman, Natalie B. 2020. "This Is Emergency Remote Teaching, Not Just Online Teaching." *Education Week*. March 30. www.edweek.org/ew/articles/2020/03/30/this-is-emergency-remote-teaching-not-just.html.

Minahan, Jessica. 2020. "Maintaining Connections, Reducing Anxiety While School Is Closed. An Educational Leadership Special Report." *A New Reality: Getting Remote Learning Right* 77: 22–27. www.ascd.org/publications/educational-leadership/summer20/vol77/num10/Maintaining-Connections,-Reducing-Anxiety-While-School-Is-Closed.aspx.

Minor, Cornelius. 2018. *We Got This: Equity, Access, and the Quest to Be Who Our Students Need Us to Be*. Portsmouth, NH: Heinemann.

Mitchell, Corey. 2020. "English-Learners May Be Left Behind as Remote Learning Becomes 'New Normal.'" *Education Week*. March 14. http://blogs.edweek.org/edweek/learning-the-language/2020/03/coronavirus_english_learners_digital_divide.html.

Morrell, Ernest. 2012. "Teachers as Critical Researchers: An Empowering Model for Urban Education." In *The Critical Qualitative Research Reader*, edited by Shirley Steinberg and Gaile Cannella, 364–79. New York: Peter Lang.

Mraz, Kristine. 2020. "Launching Units to Support a Year Like No Other." www.kristimraz.com/2020/07/23/launching-units-to-support-a-year-like-no-other/.

———. 2020. "A Handbook for Play in the Virtual/Distanced Space." www.kristimraz.com/2020/07/23/launching-units-to-support-a-year-like-no-other/.

Mraz, Kristine, Allison Porcelli, and Cheryl Tyler. *Purposeful Play.* Portsmouth, NH: Heinemann.

Muhammad, Gholdy. 2020. *Cultivating Genius: An Equity Framework for Culturally and Historically Responsive Literacy.* New York: Scholastic.

Muhtaris, Katie, and Kristen Ziemke. 2015. *Amplify: Digital Teaching and Learning in the K–6 Classroom.* Portsmouth, NH: Heinemann.

———. 2019. *Read the World: Rethinking Literacy for Empathy and Action in a Digital Age.* Portsmouth, NH: Heinemann.

National School Climate Center. 2007. "The School Climate Challenge: Narrowing the Gap Between School Climate Research and School Climate Policy, Practice Guidelines, and Teacher Education Policy." www.schoolclimate.org/themes/schoolclimate/assets/pdf/policy/school-climate-challenge-web.pdf.

Ness, Molly. *End Book Deserts* (Podcast). www.endbookdeserts.com/podcast.

Newhouse, Kara. 2020. "Four Core Priorities for Trauma-Informed Distance Learning." April 6. https://www.kqed.org/mindshift/55679/four-core-priorities-for-trauma-informed-distance-learning.

OCLC. 2020. "REALM Project Test 2 Results Available." July 20. www.webjunction.org/news/webjunction/test2-results.html.

O'Connell, Sue. (@SueOConnellMath). 2020. "Virtual manipulatives provide great visuals for math concepts." Twitter, July 13, 10:09 a.m. https://twitter.com/SueOConnellMath/status/1282723862409609216.

O'Kane, Caitlin. 2020. "Librarian Uses Drones to Deliver Books to Kids Stuck at Home Due to Coronavirus." CBS News. www.cbsnews.com/news/librarian-uses-drone-to-deliver-books-to-kids-stuck-at-home-due-to-coronavirus/?fbclid=IwAR1yIIk9LN44yrIg2IwLncR_ISWwdtc9o747UvqYsoFWQW1_D6hlveiApe0.

Oueini, Hanane, Rima Bahous, and Mona Nabhani. 2008. "Impact of Read-Aloud in the Classroom: A Case Study." *The Reading Matrix* 8 (1): 139–57.

Paley, Vivian. 2000. *White Teacher*, 2nd ed. Cambridge, MA: Harvard University Press.

Parker, Kim. 2020. "#31DaysIBPOC: We Begin, Again." May 1. https://drkimparker.org/2020/05/01/31daysibpoc-we-begin/.

Rappolt-Schlichtmann, Gabrielle. 2020. "Distance Learning: 6 UDL Best Practices for Online Learning." Understood.org. March 18. www.understood.org/en/school-learning/for-educators/universal-design-for-learning/video-distance-learning-udl-best-practices.

Reich, Justin. 2020a. "Online Learning in the Age of COVID-19." *TeachLab with Justin Reich* (Podcast). April 10. https://teachlabpodcast.com/episodes/online-learning-in-the-age-of-covid19-s1!ff245.

———. 2020b. "Remote Learning Guidance from State Education Agencies with Martin West." *TeachLab with Justin Reich* (Podcast). April 20. https://teachlabpodcast.com/episodes/remote-learning-guidance-from-state-education-s1!888e4.

Reich, Justin, Christopher J. Buttimer, Alison Fang, Garron Hillaire, Kelley Hirsch, Laura R. Larke, Joshua Littenberg-Tobias, et al. 2020. "Remote Learning Guidance from State Education Agencies During the COVID-19 Pandemic: A First Look." *EdArXiv*. April 2. https://edarxiv.org/437e2.

Rosales, John. 2018. "The Racist Beginnings of Standardized Testing from Grade School to College, Students of Color Have Suffered the Effects of Biased Testing." *NEA Today Magazine* (Spring). www.nea.org/home/73288.htm.

Rosenshine, Barak. 2012. "Principals of Instruction: Research-Based Strategies that All Teachers Should Know." *American Educator* (Spring). www.aft.org/sites/default/files/periodicals/Rosenshine.pdf.

Serravallo, Jennifer. 2010. *Teaching Reading in Small Groups*. Portsmouth, NH: Heinemann.

———. 2015. *The Reading Strategies Book*. Portsmouth, NH: Heinemann.

———. 2017. *The Writing Strategies Book*. Portsmouth, NH: Heinemann.

———. 2019. *Understanding Texts & Readers*. Portsmouth, NH: Heinemann.

———. 2020. *A Teacher's Guide to Reading Conferences*. Portsmouth, NH: Heinemann.

Simmons, Dena. 2020. "Why COVID-19 Is Our Equity Check. An Educational Leadership Special Report." *A New Reality: Getting Remote Learning Right* 77: 51–53. www.ascd.org/publications/educational_leadership/summer20/vol77/num10/Why_COVID-19_Is_Our_Equity_Check.aspx.

Souto-Manning, Mariana, Carmen I. Lugo Llerena, Jessica Martell, Abigail Salas Maguire, and Alicia Arce-Boardman. 2018. *No More Culturally Irrelevant Teaching.* Portsmouth, NH: Heinemann.

Souto-Manning, Mariana, and Jessica Martell. 2016. *Reading, Writing, and Talk: Inclusive Teaching Strategies for Diverse Learners, K–2.* New York: Teachers College Press.

Spaulding, C. 2020. "Books Distributed at MPS Lunch Sites." www.muskogeephoenix.com/news/schools/books-distributed-at-mps-lunch-sites/article_e8ba3567-845a-56a6-9acf-8d3c3a85fda8.html.

Stewart, Nikita. 2020. "She's 10, Homeless and Eager to Learn. But She Has No Internet." *New York Times.* April 13. www.nytimes.com/2020/03/26/nyregion/new-york-homeless-students-coronavirus.html.

Therrien, William J. 2004. "Fluency and Comprehension Gains as a Result of Repeated Reading: A Meta-Analysis." *Remedial and Special Education* 25 (4): 252–61. https://journals.sagepub.com/doi/abs/10.1177/07419325040250040801.

Venet, Alex Shevrin. 2016. "Building Empathetic Relationships with the Parents of Your Most Challenging Student." *Edutopia.* July 12. www.edutopia.org/discussion/building-empathetic-relationships-parents-your-most-challenging-student.

Wickham Hurst, Kelly. 2020. "What If Quarantine Homeschooling Is Better for Black Children?" https://medium.com/@kellywickham/what-if-quarantine-homeschooling-is-better-for-black-children-d8706caf5c35.

Wiggins, Grant, and Jay McTighe. 1998. *Understanding by Design.* Alexandria, VA: Association for Supervision and Curriculum Development.

Wolf, Maryanne. 2018. *Reader Come Home: The Reading Brain in a Digital World.* New York: HarperCollins.

———. 2020. "Deep Comprehension and Digital Texts: Jennifer Serravallo and Dr. Maryanne Wolf." *Heinemann Blog.* April. https://blog.heinemann.com/on-the-podcast-deep-comprehension-and-digital-texts-with-jennifer-serravallo-and-dr.-maryanne-wolf.